Criminal Law Homicide

Criminal Law Homicide

Degrees Of Murder And Defenses

Adeyemi Oshunrinade

authorHOUSE®

AuthorHouse™
1663 Liberty Drive
Bloomington, IN 47403
www.authorhouse.com
Phone: 1 (800) 839-8640

Published by AuthorHouse 04/09/2015

ISBN: 978-1-5049-0144-4 (sc)
ISBN: 978-1-5049-0143-7 (e)

Table of Contents

Dedication

TO MY WIFE

MARIA D. FERNANDEZ PEREZ

Introduction

The United States Constitution values the criminal law and fair justice, when under the Fifth and the Sixth Amendments it made clear that, no person shall be held to answer for a capital, or otherwise infamous crime, unless there is a presentment or indictment by a grand jury except, in certain circumstances as indicated in the Fifth Amendment. That in all criminal prosecutions, the accused be afforded a speedy and a public trial under an impartial jury of the jurisdiction concerned and that the accused be informed of the nature and cause of the charge: to be informed of the witnesses against him; to have compulsory process of obtaining witnesses in his favor and also to have the assistance of a counsel in his defense.

The sometimes harsh nature of the criminal justice and the idea of sentencing have made many to wonder whether "punishment" as the word is normally used is meant as a retributive measure of dealing with the offender for crime committed or as a deterrence from the commission of future crimes. Others believed that punishment for crime committed help rehabilitate the offender while some think it is a way of incapacitating the offender and keeping such people where they belong- the prison.

Irrespective of individual notion of punishment, the most important value is that there is a process in place in the United States as in other civilized nations, recognized and constitutionally respected for dealing with crimes and for delivering justice, based on settled criminal law, under both the State and Federal justice system. There is no doubt that the imposition of punishment, its severity, efficacy, or its futility, is all a result of legislative policy. Such policy is intended for the purpose of putting in place a standard of criminal justice without which it is inevitable that, each decision maker may impose punishment as he sees fit causing chaos and unfair justice. Nonetheless, criminal sentencing can be used to serve as retribution or the exact payment for crime committed-"an eye for an eye." It can be used as a *deterrence* to prevent commission of future crimes and to discourage others from committing it or other crimes. It may also be used as a *denunciation*, and condemnation of the defendant or as a means to re-enforce his moral standards as a reassurance to the society. Another purpose of criminal sentencing is *incapacitation*- serving as a tool for keeping the offender away from the public during the term of his sentence thereby, minimizing danger to the law-abiding citizens. Finally, it may serve as a tool for *rehabilitation* or reformation of the offender whereby, he becomes sober and able to reflect on his wrongdoings, make changes, and become a better citizen.

With the book, I carefully carved *homicide law* out of criminal law, by focusing on court cases dealing with homicide and by asking thought provoking questions that provides better understanding and knowledge of the crime of homicide, as a branch of criminal law.

Chapter One
Procedure Of Criminal Justice

The prior Investigation: On learning of the commission of a crime, officers are deployed to the scene of the crime to gather information that will help make an arrest. In trying to solve the crime, the police may gather information to determine whether a crime was committed and if so, who committed the crime. They may also collect evidence to help determine the offender' guilt and information on how to locate the offender so he can be taken into custody. Other investigative activities may include: interviewing victims at the scene of the crime; interviewing witnesses who may have seen the crime in progress; interviewing of suspects and persons of interest; examination of the crime scene for possible incriminating evidence; information gathering from informants; gathering of arrest records from departmental database; surveillance of the crime scene; and searching for both direct and physical evidence at the crime scene. The pre-arrest investigation may also be reactive, proactive, and prosecutorial in nature however, all have one end, which is to have enough and convincing evidence for an arrest.

The Arrest: On determining there is a probable cause to make an arrest based on information and evidence gathered, the police may go forward to make an arrest. The arrest process may sometimes involve the use of force in order to place the offender in police custody before charges are made but depending on the jurisdiction, the police may be asked to first detain the offender and then release him upon the issue of a *citation*, requiring him to appear in court at a later date determined by the court. The purpose is to allow him to respond to whatever charge is brought against him however, it is important to note that such *citation* is issued only on minor offenses.

In situations where there is no need for immediate arrest, an *arrest warrant* or court order may be obtained prior to detaining the offender however, to obtain such a warrant, there must be a probable cause to believe the offender actually committed the crime. Arrest warrants are issued in most cases by the magistrates and are useful in cases where the offender: resides or is found in another jurisdiction different from where the crime was committed; where the offender cannot be located; where the officers making arrest may need to enter into another' dwelling in order to make an arrest; and in a situation where the police sought the advice of a prosecutor before deciding to make an arrest.

The Booking: On completion of arrest, the next step is to book the arrestee; normally this takes place at the police station, a jail or some holding facility designated for booking. The arrestee is also photographed and fingerprinted for record keeping. An arrestee booked on a misdemeanor may be allowed to post a bail for immediate release depending on the jurisdiction. In such cases, the arrestee is allowed to post a specified amount in cash as bail money and he agrees to appear in court at a designated date.

After- Arrest- Information Gathering: Usually the police may decide to conduct further investigation and gather more evidence after the arrest. These may include gathering information that are not readily available before the arrest such as: seeking eyewitnesses to identify the arrestee from a lineup photos of other individuals including photo of the arrestee; the arrestee may be brought for a show-up to see if the eyewitness is able to identify him; DNA samples may be taken from the arrestee for comparison to ones taken at the crime scene; and the arrestee may be questioned further to determine his connection to related crimes.

The Charge: Before the charge is brought the followings must be established: (1) the arresting officer must show probable cause based on his investigation that the arrest is warranted; (2) the police review of the decision to arrest before charges are brought; prosecutorial review prior to the charge; and ongoing prosecutorial review after filing the charge.

The above mentioned are necessary for the court to determine whether the charges are proper or else the court may decide not to move forward with the case. For example, during a pre-filing police screening, internal review may reveal charges should not be brought at the level recommended by the arresting officer and the police supervisor may decide that based on the review, there is a need to either reduce or increase the charges. In such cases, the review may show a lack or insufficient evidence to increase the charges to the level recommended and as a result, it would be proper to go with a lesser charge.

The prosecutor while conducting his pre-filing review must also decide whether the evidence is sufficient enough to bring charges. In cases involving misdemeanors and felonies, charges are not brought until the approval of the prosecutor who must properly screen the evidence to make sure there is probable cause to make the arrest and bring charges. The prosecutor may decide not to bring charges if the evidence is insufficient or where he determines there is implication of the *due process*. Other reasons may be based on the nature of the arrest for example, where the arrest is unjust, where alternative prosecution is in place and where a diversion program is in place that enables the arrestee to enter into rehab and avoid conviction.

In cases where the decision is to charge, the prosecutor works to determine the level of the charge based on the evidence provided for example, a felony charge may be reduced to a lesser charge or a misdemeanor if based on supporting evidence the penalty of a higher charge is so severe for the nature of the crime committed. Even though, charges may have been brought, this does not stop the prosecutor from conducting a post-filing review where he checks the facts of the case and determine whether a charge is justified. If based on the post-filing review he determines the charges are unjustified he may recommend a dismissal by filing a motion not to prosecute the case. On the other hand, if the prosecutor considers the charges too high, he can file a motion to reduce the charges.

The Complaint: The next stage is to file the actual complaint, this usually takes place if based on the pre-charge review it is determined that a charge is warranted and proper. The charging instrument in this case is termed the *complaint*, which is usually filed with the magistrate. Throughout the proceedings, the complaint serves as the charging instrument in a misdemeanor however, in a felony it serves to set forth the charges before the magistrate and later replaced by an indictment at trial. The complaint usually describes the allegations including time, place, and manner of crime for which the accused is indicted. It states what criminal law is violated and at the end the complainant signs the instrument under oath.

Magistrate Screening: On establishing the complaint, the magistrate then makes his own determination by screening the arrest instrument and warrant to ensure there is a legal ground for holding the arrestee and keeping him in custody. If the magistrate sees a probable cause for holding the arrestee, he may remain in custody but if probable cause is lacking the magistrate may order him released.

The Initial Appearance: On satisfaction of the above mentioned procedures, the accused then makes his first appearance before the magistrate; this is called the *preliminary appearance* in some jurisdictions and it is always required that the accused be presented to court in a prompt fashion. In some jurisdictions a time limit of 24 hours is set for the accused to be presented before the court after arrest and detention. Other jurisdictions allow for a 48 hours pre-appearance detention.

On appearance, the magistrate then certifies the accused making sure he is the person named in the complaint he is informed of the charges against him and his rights. Most importantly he is notified of his right to remain silent that anything he says may be used against him in the court of law. A defendant in a misdemeanor case is usually not entitled to a preliminary hearing or a grand jury review but on the other hand, a defendant charged with a felony gets a preliminary hearing and is informed of the next step in the process including the date for the hearing however, he may choose to waive the hearing. The defendant is also notified of his right to have an attorney represent him and if unable to provide one, he is informed of his right to a court appointed counsel. Depending on the jurisdiction, a court appointed counsel, may not be available for one charged with a low level misdemeanor if the end result does not include incarceration on conviction. Otherwise, one charged with a felony or a serious misdemeanor is entitled to appointed counsel.

During appearance, the magistrate may set bail to allow the defendant leave custody pending the final decision on the charges against him. A bails determination must be made in a felony or serious misdemeanor charge however, in a low level misdemeanor a bail may not be necessary because misdemeanors cases, the accused will have posted a bail at the police station or enter a guilty plea at the initial appearance and sentenced accordingly. The defendant required to post bail, may post money in cash however, other alternative forms of bail may be used such as: release on personal recognizance and promise to return to court; promise to forfeit certain amount in cash on failure to return to court; release upon restrictions on travel and association (court may seize defendant travel document) for assurance; and defendant may choose to forfeit 10% of bail amount should he fail to reappear.

Depending on the severity of the crime, the magistrate may refuse bail if the defendant is considered a flight risk for example, the court may refuse bail for one charged with multiple homicide because of the seriousness of the charge or because such defendant is considered a danger to the society if released temporarily on bail. In such situation, the court may determine that no condition of bail will prevent such defendant from committing another crime.

Preliminary Examination: In most jurisdictions, the felony defendant has the right to a preliminary hearings, this takes place a week or two depending on the circumstances of release of the defendant. A defendant without a pre-trial release gets his hearing within a week or two and if released within few weeks however, a defendant may decide to waive such hearing and therefore, move his case to trial; in such cases the defendant may have elected to plead guilty to charges against him and avoid a lengthy trial.

In a situation where there is a preliminary hearing, the magistrate must properly look at the evidence against the defendant and determine the existence of a probable cause to charge the defendant for the said crime. Evidence to be looked at must include witness testimony and presence in court rather than mere affidavits.

Evidence screening by the Grand Jury: In most jurisdictions to indict a defendant based on a felony charge, the prosecution must present the evidence before a grand jury[1] charged, to review it and determine whether based on evidence presented there is probable cause to justify a trial and issue an indictment. The grand jury is made of private citizens who come from different professional backgrounds. Traditionally, the grand jury is comprise of 23 persons with the vote of a majority needed to issue an indictment however, some jurisdictions now use a grand jury of 12 persons. The meeting of the grand jury takes place in a closed session where the prosecution presents evidence and in such session, the defendant is not required to be present or present evidence. During the session, prosecution evidence is reviewed by the grand jury. An indictment will issue only if based on the evidence, a majority of the jurors determine that evidence presented is sufficient. The charge is thereafter indicated in the instrument of indictment as a *true bill* otherwise, charges are dropped if the grand jury determines the evidence as presented by the prosecution is insufficient.

Filing the Indictment: After issue of indictment by the grand jury, a charge is then filed with the trial court replacing the complaint as the accusatory instrument. Normally, the prosecutor representing the county or state where the crime originated files the charge.

Arraignment of the Accused: The next step in the process after the indictment is to bring the defendant before the court, he is informed of the charges and he is asked how he would like to plea to the charges whether guilty or not guilty. In a felony case, a guilty plea[2] may be entered by the defendant based on prior arrangement and agreement between the defendant's counsel and the prosecution; this may happen as a result of the overwhelming evidence against the defendant and

---

[1] Majority of States and the Federal system require a grand jury indictment for all felony prosecutions; such States are referred to as "*indictment jurisdictions*". In some other States, indictments are issued only for the most severe cases such as cases involving life sentence, death sentence and more; they are called "*limited indictment jurisdictions*".

[2] This is considered a way of disposing felony indictments and is applied as a tool for preventing lengthy trials in cases that could have gone to trial had the defendant pled not guilty. It is applied in all jurisdictions and it is used also in misdemeanors however, the plea deal rate is as high or higher as to misdemeanor charges.

if it is unlikely the defendant will have a lighter sentence if subject to a full trial, defendant counsel may advise on taking a plea deal to avoid a lengthy trial and get a lighter sentence for his client.

A defendant charged with a felony after a pre-charge review, may have his sentence reduced to a misdemeanor if he chooses to enter a plea deal; or a defendant facing multiple charges may have his charge consolidated to a single or lesser charge, based on the concession to enter a guilty plea offered by the prosecution however, a plea deal takes place only after some rounds of negotiation and bargaining between the defense counsel and the prosecution.

The pretrial Motion: During the pretrial motion, the defendant may raise questions attacking the evidence presented by the prosecution, he may try to dispute the charges or label it frivolous based on insufficient evidence or claim that the evidence is tainted as a result of the way it was handled (suppression of evidence). The defendant may use such motion to ask that charges be dismissed due to constitutional violation of rights of the defendant or because the prosecution failed to follow the normal criminal procedure before indictment by the grand jury.

Actual Trial: The trial is the next step in a criminal charge whenever negotiation between the defendant and prosecution for a plea deal or guilty plea fail to materialize. In a criminal trial all accused are considered innocent until proven guilty and the prosecution must show proof beyond reasonable doubt that the defendant did commit the crime for which he is charged. The defendant has the right not to take the stand in his own defense and all evidence obtained in a manner proscribed by law including incriminating statements of the defendant are inadmissible. These requirements are necessary in order to offer the defendant a fair trial since a criminal sentence is considered a life-changing event that may affect the defendant for his entire life. To avoid sentencing the innocent, precautions are taken to ensure the trial is fair and that the prosecution proves his case beyond reasonable doubt.

In all felony cases, the defendant has the right to a trial by jury and for misdemeanors carrying sentence of more than six months. Usually, there is a jury of 12 persons however some jurisdictions have jury of 6 members for misdemeanors. In the case a defendant decides to waive the right to a trial by jury, a bench trial is usually the next option; and in order to convict or acquit a defendant in a felony or misdemeanor, the jury verdict must be unanimous. Where there is no unanimous vote or a "*hung jury*" the case is retried and there is no verdict.

The Sentencing: The next face of sentencing the defendant is a function of the court. The defendant has the right to a jury trial if other facts arise such as a prior conviction that may change the sentencing period or increase time to be served beyond statutory limit. The facts are presented to the jury who must review and the prosecution must prove beyond reasonable doubt, that such a sentencing is warranted for the jury to render verdict and certify to the court for sentencing. Criminal sentencing may take the form of financial sanctions such as a fine or restitution, which the defendant must pay to the plaintiff or the court. The defendant may also be placed on probation during which he must not commit another crime or violate the probation order; he may also have unsupervised release or placed under house arrest during which he is not allowed to leave the court ordered destination. Finally, he may be subject to incarceration in jail for lighter sentences or prison for longer ones.

In some cases, the sentence to be served by one convicted is determined by the law such as where the legislature has set a standard for prosecuting the accused and the punishment that fits the crime.[3]

The Appeal: In all criminal cases, the convicted defendant has the right to appeal. The defendant may bring his appeal before the State Court of Appeal or the intermediate appellate court to review the decision of the magistrate court. For a State with no such court, the appeal is forwarded to the State Supreme Court for appellate review. Most appeals are linked to felony convictions and those based on guilty pleas are linked to sentencing challenges for example, where the defendant feels the punishment for the crime was too harsh even though, a guilty plea was entered.

Most appeals are based on the trial process; the convicted defendant may challenge how the judge handled the case or how the jury was charged before presenting the case to the judge for sentencing. Another ground may be based on the admission of evidence, insufficiency of evidence or the lack of it.

After-Conviction Rights: After all appeals, the convicted defendant may use other remedies to challenge his conviction for example, he may challenge the conviction based on constitutional ground by claiming the police had no warrant or engaged in unreasonable searches while looking for evidence in his premises. For example, in April of 2011 Cleve Foster, a convicted murderer, asked the court to hold his execution minutes after eating his last meal and was scheduled to be executed. He claimed *ineffective counsel*. The judge agreed and decided to review his conviction based on new evidence presented claiming his innocence of the crime.

---

[3] For a complete reading on sentencing, see **Wayne R. Lafave**, Modern Criminal Law: Cases, Comments and Questions, fourth edition 2001 p. 12

Notes: Read the questions below, find the right answer and write your analysis of the case in the space provided, based on how you arrived at the correct answer from the choices given.

Capital One Bank had a increase in robberies at its main branch in Baltimore. The board decided to hire George, a retired sniper to protect the bank. George received orders to shoot if deemed necessary to prevent a robbery.

Days after George began work at the bank, Curtis entered the bank, pointed a gun at the cashier and demanded all bills in the drawer. The moment George saw Curtis point a gun at the cashier, George fired and killed Curtis instantly.

Is George guilty of any criminal offense?

    (A) **No crime if George reasonably believed shooting was necessary to stop a potential felony**

    (B) **George is guilty of voluntary Manslaughter, because he employed a deadly weapon to protect a private property**

    (C) **Voluntary manslaughter, since George did not warn Curtis before firing**

    (D) **George is guilty of murder, if he deliberately aimed to kill Curtis.**

Notes:

Notes:

Notes: Read the question below, find your answer in the choices provided and include your analysis of how you arrived at the right choice.

Andrew met with Chris his childhood friend and asked him to help kill Betty by shooting her. Andrew paid Chris for the job and late at night two days after the transaction, Chris slipped into Betty's home through a window opening but realized shooting her might wake up the entire household. He decided to set Betty's bed on fire instead and Betty died of smoke inhalation.

Is Andrew responsible for the murder of Betty?

   (A) Andrew is responsible because he conspired with Chris
   (B) Andrew is responsible because he masterminded the homicide
   (C) Andrew is not responsible because he did not enter Betty's home
   (D) No because Andrew set no fire on Betty's mattress.

Notes:

Chapter Two

The Crime Of Homicide

Mental State Classification And The "Born Alive Rule"

HUGHES V. STATE

Court Of Criminal Appeals Of Oklahoma, 868 P.2D 730 (1994)

The events in this case began On August 2, 1990. The appellant, Treva LaNan Hughes, while intoxicated and driving, collided with another vehicle. The driver of the other vehicle Reesa Poole was nine months pregnant at the time and expected to deliver in four days. Due to the collision, Poole's stomach hit the steering wheel of her car with a force that caused the steering wheel to break. Poole was taken to a hospital where an emergency cesarean section was performed. At delivery, the only sign of life the baby had was an extremely slow heartbeat. A pediatrician tried resuscitation efforts, which failed.

Hughes was convicted of First Degree Manslaughter after a jury trial in the District Court of Oklahoma County under 21 O.S.1981, § 711(1), which defines ("[h]omicide as manslaughter in the first degree… When perpetrated without a design to effect death by a person while engaged in the commission of a misdemeanor"). The jury also found Hughes guilty of Driving Under the Influence While Involved in a Personal Injury Accident. Hughes was sentenced to eight-year in prison for the manslaughter conviction and a six-month suspended sentence for driving under the influence.

Hughes asked for a reversal of her manslaughter conviction on the basis of the common law "born alive" rule. Because Oklahoma has neither altered nor abolished this remnant of the common law, it remains in effect pursuant to 22 O.S.1981, § 9.[4] Under the "born alive" rule, "[a] child cannot be the subject of homicide until its complete expulsion from the body of the mother, and must be alive and have independent existence."[5] Hughes claims that the fetus Ms. Poole was carrying

---

[4] See also *Eliot v. Mills, 335 P.2d. 1104, 1111(Okla. Cr.1959)*
[5] *Warren, Warren on Homicide § 55 (1938)*

was not born alive and therefore, its death cannot be a homicide. The court decided to reject the common law approach and concluded that whether or not it is ultimately born alive, an unborn fetus that was viable at the time of injury is a "human being" which may be the subject of a homicide under 21 O.S.1981, § 691 ("Homicide is the killing of one human being by another")

The dissent adopts the State's position that the "born alive" rule would not prohibit a manslaughter conviction in this case because the fetus in question was born alive. The court indicated that its decision to reject the "born alive" rule was based on its origins, history and purpose. Common law authorities refer to the born alive rule as early as the 1300's.[6] The court reiterated that, the born alive rule was necessitated by the state of medical technology in earlier centuries, and expressed that the better rule must be that the Infliction, of prenatal injuries resulting in the death of a viable fetus, before or after it is born, is homicide. If a person were to commit violence against a pregnant woman and destroy the fetus within her,[7] "we would not want the death of the fetus to go unpunished. We believe that our criminal law should extend its protection to viable fetuses *(1984)*.

In conclusion, the court rejected the born alive rule and held that a viable human fetus is a "human being" against whom a homicide as defined in section 691 may be committed. In its ruling, the court agreed that the fetus suffered fatal injuries as a result of Hughes's drunk driving and that it was viable. However, Hughes may not be convicted for the fetus's death because, she could not have foreseen the court's decision to abolish the born alive rule and effectively render her actions homicidal. The court then, applied its ruling prospectively to those homicides, which occur after its date.

Based on the court's opinion, Hughes' judgment and sentence for first-degree manslaughter, was REVERSED and REMANDED with instructions to DISMISS. Hughes' judgment and sentence for driving under the influence while involved in a personal injury accident was AFFIRMED.

NOTE: Please locate the case from other sources using the case number above. Read the entire case as well as the court's opinion to help you answer the questions below.

---

[6] Forsythe, Homicide of the Unborn Child: *The Born Alive Rule and other Legal Anachronisms, 21 Valparaiso L.R. 563, 581 (1987)*

[7] Oklahoma statute 21 O.S. 1981, § 713 "the willful killing of an unborn quick child by any injury committed upon the person of the mother of such child is manslaughter in the first degree." Also, in *Hooks v. State, 862 P.2d (Okl. Cr. 1993)* the defendant was convicted under section 713 for killing an unborn viable fetus by fatally injuring the mother.

Notes and Questions

[1] Is it sound argument to conclude the child was dead upon delivery? Notice that the court's decision to dismiss the conviction of manslaughter relates to that determination however, all evidence point to the fact that but for the accident, the fetus would have survived. Should the born alive rule have applied even though, all facts indicate that Hughes was involved in a misdemeanor leading to the action that caused injury to the mother and the unborn child?

Notes:

[2] Notice the court admitted that difficulty of proving causation is not a reason for denying criminal liability. What motivated the court to relief Hughes of the manslaughter charge, despite the court's willingness to do away with the born alive rule? Explain your answer in the space provided below.

Notes:

[3] Should a mother be held accountable for injuries sustained by her unborn child as a result of the mother's action before birth? This issue was put to test in *State v. Cornelius, 152 Wis.2d 272, 282-83, 448 N.W.2d 434, 438 (1989)*; where the defendant was charged with homicide for the death of an unborn child, as a result of accident caused by defendant's intoxicated driving. The court upheld the homicide charge on the conclusion that, the unborn child qualified as a 'human being' within the statute because it was alive at birth. Moreover, the child was born alive but died due to injuries sustained in utero.

Many have argued that such statutes and homicide charge not be extended broadly to include every action in which a defendant has engaged in self destructive behavior during pregnancy that may result in injury to the child. For example, under such interpretation, a woman could be criminally liable for smoking or abusing prescribed medications during her pregnancy. Also, she could be liable criminally for failing to seek proper prenatal care while pregnant if the child becomes injured as a result of the mother's inaction. Public policy disapproves of such criminal sanctions on the belief it may hinder would be mothers from seeking prenatal care for fear that, any act or omission on their part, may lead to criminal prosecution should the child be born with injuries.

[3] Note- an unborn child may be subject of a child abuse case for action taken by the mother during pregnancy. In **Whitner v. State, 328 S.C. 1(1997)** holding that a viable fetus is a 'child' within the statute, a mother was charged for ingesting crack cocaine during the third trimester of pregnancy, when her child was born with cocaine metabolites in its system. Whitner argues that the statute as it stands does not include viable fetus and giving it such interpretation, may lead to results not intended by the legislature. She claims if 'child' is meant to include viable fetuses then, every action by a pregnant woman legal or illegal, causing danger or likely to cause danger to a fetus, would constitute unlawful neglect under the statute. For example, a woman might be prosecuted under section 20-7-50 for smoking or drinking during pregnancy. Whitner asserts these 'absurd' results could not have been intended by the legislature and, therefore, the statute should not be construed to include viable fetuses. The court responded as follows to Whitner's claims:

The court disagreed for a number of reasons. First, the same arguments against the statute can be made whether or not the child has been born. After the birth of a child, a parent can be prosecuted under section 20-7-50 for an action that is likely to endanger the child without regard to whether the action is illegal in itself. For example, a parent who drinks excessively could, under certain circumstances, be guilty of child neglect or endangerment even though the underlying act-consuming alcoholic beverages-is itself legal. Obviously, the legislature did not think it 'absurd' to allow prosecution of parents for such otherwise legal acts when the acts actually or potentially endanger the 'life, health or comfort' of the parents' born children. The court saw no reason such a result should be rendered absurd by the mere fact the child at issue is a viable fetus.

Based on facts, "Whitner admits to having ingested crack cocaine during the third trimester of her pregnancy, which caused her child to be born with cocaine in its system. Although the precise effect of maternal crack use during pregnancy are somewhat unclear, it is well documented and within the realm of public knowledge that such use can cause serious harm to the viable unborn child."[8] All facts show that Whitner endangered the life, health, and comfort of her child...

"We do not think any fundamental right of Whitner's or any right at all, for that matter-is implicated under the present scenario. It strains belief for Whitner to argue that using crack cocaine during pregnancy is encompassed within the constitutionally recognized right of privacy. The opinion indicated that the use of crack cocaine is illegal, and there is no argument, that laws criminalizing the use of crack cocaine are themselves unconstitutional. If the State wishes to impose additional criminal penalties on pregnant women who engage in the already illegal conduct because of the effect the conduct has on the viable fetus, it may do so. The fact of pregnancy does not elevate the use of crack cocaine to the lofty status of a fundamental right.

The court's interpretation of section 20-7-50 does not impose any burden on Whitner's right to carry her child to term. ... During her pregnancy after the fetus-attained viability, Whitner enjoyed the same freedom to use cocaine that she enjoyed earlier in and predating her pregnancy-none whatsoever. South Carolina child abuse and endangerment statute as applied to the case does not restrict Whitner's freedom in any way that it was not already restricted. The State's imposition of an additional penalty when a pregnant woman with a viable fetus engages in the already proscribed behavior does not burden a woman's right to carry her pregnancy to term; but, the additional penalty simply recognizes that a third party (the viable fetus or newborn child) is harmed by the behavior.

The court ruled that Section 20-7-50 does not burden Whitner's right to carry her pregnancy to term or any other privacy right. Therefore, there was no violation of the Due Process Clause of the Fourteenth Amendment.

---

[8] Joseph J. Volpe, M.D., *Effect of Cocaine Use on the Fetus, 327 NEW ENG. J. MED. 399 (1992)*

[4] 'In *People v. Chavez 77 Cal.App.2d 621, 176 P.2d 92 (1947)* the defendant was convicted of manslaughter for the death of her child. Based on her testimony, the baby dropped from her womb into the toilet bowl. She cut the umbilical cord but failed to tie it. Her baby was found dead the following day…

On appeal, the defendant claimed the child was not born alive, that the idea of live birth was due to speculation. The court disagreed and affirmed the conviction, based on doctor's testimony and evidence that the baby was born alive. (See *People v. Chavez, for the entire case*)

[5] Note that in some jurisdictions the unlawful killing of an unborn fetus is deemed manslaughter. In *State v. Shaw, 219 So.2d 49 (Fla.1969)*; The Florida statute states: "The willful killing of an unborn quick child, by an injury to the mother of such child which would be murder if it resulted in the death of such mother, shall be deemed manslaughter." What is the rationale behind such rule? What happens if it would be manslaughter if it resulted in the death of such mother? Imagine a scenario where death of the mother is as a result of *passion*, will the same rule apply in such jurisdiction, so that death of the unborn child would be manslaughter? Please explain your answer with analysis.

[6] It has been held also that "death occurring to a child because an assault on the mother before death of the child is sufficient to sustain a murder conviction where the child was born alive, had spontaneous respiration and heart rate, and survived 12 hours before dying from a condition caused by premature birth due to the assault." *Ranger v. State, 249 Ga. 315, 290 S.E.2d 63 (1982)*; Do you consider a murder conviction proper in such a case? What about an argument that the defendant did not intend to injure the child but the mother? Or that during the confrontation, the mother, pulled a knife on the defendant, such that the defendant acted in self –defense, causing death of the child. Will that be enough to exculpate defendant?

[7] 'Fetuses which are the victims of a criminal blow or wound upon their mother, and are subsequently born alive, but die by reason of a chain of circumstances caused by such blow or wound, may be victims of murder.' *State v. Anderson, 135 N.J.Super. 423, 343 A.2d 505 (1975)*[9]

---

[9] Ref. Rollin M. Perkins, *Criminal Law and Procedure supra, note (a) at P.48.*

Notes: Carefully read the following question and pick your answer from the choices. Explain why you think your choice is the right answer in the space provided, using facts from the case.

Carl wanted to kill Carol, he shot at Carol and missed but the bullet hit Brian instead. Fortunately, Brian was only slightly graced by the bullet. Enraged, Brian picked a baseball bat he found nearby and beat Carol, thinking it was Carol that shot him.

Did Carl commit the attempted murder of Brian?

   (A) Yes because Carl attempted to kill Carol, therefore his intent may transfer to Brian
   (B) Yes because Carl acted with premeditation and malice towards Carol
   (C) No because the bullet only graced Brian
   (D) No because Carol did not intend to kill Brian.

Notes:

Notes: Read the same fact in the question above and make the right choice from the question below.

Did Brian commit the battery of Carol?

(A) Yes, because Brian intentionally beat Carol

(B) Yes, because Carol did nothing wrong

(C) No, if Brian acted in the heat of passion though, Carol did nothing wrong

(D) No, if Brian reasonably believed Carol had shot at him.

Chapter Three

Intentional Murder

"Heat of Passion"

In an intentional homicide, it is always a requirement to show that the defendant intended death or that he intended an act calculated such that, a person of reason should know that such act is one likely to do great bodily harm and that death occurred. Most voluntary manslaughter cases involve the intent to kill however there are cases where the defendant killed without intent, but with reckless disregard for human life. In such a case the defendant may have acted in the *heat of passion* with adequate provocation. The defendant is therefore, guilty of voluntary manslaughter and not murder if facts show he acted unintentionally without the design to kill but in the heat of passion. On the other hand, a defendant who killed intentionally in the heat of passion would be guilty of murder.

To establish heat of passion, it must be shown that at the time of the act, the reason is so disturbed or overcome by passion to an extent, which might make ordinary men of fair, average disposition liable to act irrationally without due deliberation or reflection and the action must have taken place as a result of passion rather than judgment. However, it is not every provocation or every rage that will reduce a killing from murder to manslaughter. Under the traditional heat of passion doctrine, a provoked defendant cannot have his homicide reduced to voluntary manslaughter, where the time elapsing between the provocation and the deathblow is such that a reasonable man would have cooled off. The provocation must be of such a character and so close to the act of killing that a person could be- that for a moment the defendant, could be considered as not being the author of his own understanding.

In other words, to have an intentional killing reduced to voluntary manslaughter, there must be *reasonable provocation*. The provocation must be such as to cause a reasonable man in the position of the defendant to kill but nonetheless, a reasonable man however highly provoked he may be, does not kill. Therefore, the law recognizes that one, who kills while provoked, should not get away with his crime but be guilty of the lesser crime of voluntary manslaughter instead. In essence, one who is highly provoked to kill his provoker should not be guilty of murder but at the same time, must not be allowed to get away with his crime, making his crime to fall in the category of voluntary manslaughter.

While one may be so provoked to kill and have his crime reduced from murder to voluntary manslaughter, there is a growing debate as to what actually constitutes a crime of passion or reasonable provocation. For example, one subject to a light blow may not kill and then claim reasonable provocation. Even though, this is battery, it is not enough to cause the defendant to kill.[10] However, a violent, painful blow, with fist or weapon, ordinarily will constitute reasonable provocation.[11] Even in such cases where the defendant is subject to a painful blow, the defendant may not have his homicide reduced to voluntary manslaughter if facts show the defendant struck the first blow or is responsible for the painful blow received from the provoker. In some cases, whether the homicide is reduced from murder to voluntary manslaughter may depend on the kind of weapon used in response to the provocation. For example, where the provoker used a light blow with a fist on the defendant, the defendant may not in retaliation, use a dagger in response to the light blow and have his homicide reduced to voluntary manslaughter, since the use of dagger constitutes excessive force.[12]

There are instances, where two persons are engaged in mutual combat resulting in the homicide of one of the parties, as a result of the intention formed by the defendant during the fracas. In such cases, should the defendant be guilty of murder for the homicide of the victim? In response, such homicide is considered manslaughter and not murder.[13] This may be due to the *mutual* nature of the combat and in some cases compared to provocation involved in batteries.

Where a violent assault is committed on the defendant such that he is provoked to kill, the better view has been that an unsuccessful violent assault may constitute adequate provocation leading to a homicide. For example, where the attacker fires a gun at the defendant, *Stevenson v. United States, 162 U.S. 313 (1896)*; the defendant in such extreme case may have his homicide reduced to voluntary manslaughter.

There are different views as to whether one subject to illegal arrest may be so provoked to commit murder. Some believe such an arrest might reasonably arouse passion leading to murder. Others

---

[10] *Commonwealth v. Rembiszewski, 363 Mass. 311, 293 N.E. 2d 919 (1973)* where scratches on defendant's face is insufficient provocation to kill with a deadly weapon
[11] *People v. Harris, 8 Ill.2d 431, 134 N.E. 2d 315 (1956)*
[12] *Mancini v. Director of Public Prosecutions, (1942)*
[13] *People v. Leonard, 83 Ill.2d 411 (1980), Robinson v. State, 773 So.2d 943 (Miss.App.2000)*

think a reasonable person could not be so provoked by an illegal arrest to commit a homicide. Irrespective of the views, an arrest that is carried out by a law enforcement agent or that is legal cannot constitute sufficient provocation to commit murder[14] however, there is the view that an innocent person subject to illegal arrest, might be reasonably provoked than a guilty one.

In most jurisdiction of the United States, it is settled principle of law that a husband who finds his wife in the act of committing adultery may be reasonably overcome by passion so as to kill either his wife or the lover. In such cases, he has not committed murder but rather voluntary manslaughter.[15] Likewise, a wife may be reasonably provoked on finding her husband in the act of adultery with another woman; *Scroggs v. State, 94 Ga. App. 28 (1956),* where wife killed the other woman upon discovery her of adultery, with her husband. The point to take home is that this principle of law applies to women as it does to men. Note that the rule mitigating the crime of murder to manslaughter does not extend to unmarried couples such as engaged persons, divorced persons and unmarried lovers.

The initial view is that words plus gestures alone, will not satisfy mitigating murder to voluntary manslaughter however, the rule is changing today. In many jurisdictions, words alone will do as a mitigating factor for reducing intentional murder to voluntary manslaughter. To be reasonable ground for provocation, the words must convey information of a fact, which would provoke a reasonable person. Mere insulting, abusive words, or hearsay will not do. A word of gesture such as homosexual advances that are unwanted and rejected by the defendant will do to arouse reasonable provocation and be a mitigating factor for reducing intentional killing, to voluntary manslaughter. However, a non-violent homosexual advance will not suffice. Merely "experiencing fear or hatred of gay people in response to a homosexual overture should not suffice to provoke a reasonable person to lose his or her self control and resort to deadly force."[16]

Under the ***reasonable man standard***, the fact that the defendant has peculiar mental or physical characteristics not possessed by the ordinary individual, that caused him to lose control are generally not considered as a mitigating factor for reducing his homicide to voluntary manslaughter. Likewise, the intentional killing may not be reduced to voluntary manslaughter where, because of intoxication, he loses self-control. That is to say, he is to be judged by the standard of a reasonable

[14] *State v. Madden, 61 N.J. 377, 294 A.2d 609 (1972)*
[15] *Rowland v. State, 83 Miss. 483, 35 So. 826 (1904),* where it is manslaughter when husband, upon discovery of wife committing adultery with lover, shot at lover but missed and killing the wife instead. See also, *Gonzales v. State, 546 S.W.2d 617 (Tex. Crim. App. 1977)* where it is manslaughter when husband shot lover found in bed with his wife.
[16] *Developments-Sexual Orientation and the Law, 102 Harv. L.Rev. 1547 (note 56)*

sober man. The test is usually how the victim's action affects a reasonable person, not how it affects a person with the defendant's physical characteristics.[17]

In circumstances where a reasonable person may be so provoked to lose self-control, it must be determine if the defendant was actually provoked by the victim's action so as to kill. If because he is a person of cooler temperament than the reasonable man, he was not actually provoked but killed his victim in cold blood, he is guilty of murder and the intentional killing may not be reduced to voluntary manslaughter.[18]

COOLING-OFF

Imagine the scenario of a fight between two persons; one was struck with a metal object suffering minor injuries. After the fight was broken, he went home and had lunch with his wife. Forty minutes later still mad he was struck, came back to the scene of the fight with a gun, shot the other killing him. The question is should he have his murder charge reduced to voluntary manslaughter? In most cases the answer is no. Even though, the victim's action actually provokes and reasonably provokes the defendant into a heat of passion, the laws recognize a reasonable time to cool-off and diffuse the situation. In this case, forty minutes is enough time for the passion to subside and cool off. The forty minutes in this case serves as a time lag between the provocation and infliction of the fatal wound (killing of the victim). The general view is that a provoked defendant cannot have his homicide reduced to voluntary manslaughter where there is a time lapse between the provocation and the deathblow such that, a reasonable man thus provoked would have cooled. Under the minority view, the reasonable- time test may not apply. However, if there is a reasonable and actual provocation, the defendant is only guilty of manslaughter if in fact, because of his peculiar temperament, he has not cooled off though, a reasonable man would have cooled.[19]

In the case discussed above, even though, the defendant was provoked into a passion by the strike, another event occurred which could have helped him to cool-off and avoid the killing. By having lunch with his wife, he had enough time to think about the whole event and change his mind. In most cases, what determines a reasonable cooling time may be based on the nature of

[17] *Bedder v. Director of Public Prosecutions, (1954)*
[18] *People v. Gingell, 211 Cal. 532, 296 P. 70 (1931),* where defendant suspecting his wife of adultery, decided to kill her, then found her in bed with paramour and decided to kill them both; it was held to be murder and not manslaughter.
[19] *State v. Hazlett, 16 N.D. 426, 113 N.W. 374 (1907)*

the provocation and the circumstances of the event. However the case may be, this is a question of fact for the jury to decide.

Where fact show the defendant is both reasonably and actually provoked and a reasonable man would not have cooled off in the circumstance, the defendant will not have his homicide mitigated to voluntary manslaughter 'if, because his passion subsides more quickly than those of the ordinary person, he has actually cooled off by the time he commits his deadly act.'[20]

In summary, it is clear to say that: (a) one who is found to be both reasonably and actually provoked and who reasonably and actually does not cool off, is not guilty of murder but instead voluntary manslaughter; (b) one who is actually provoked to kill, is unreasonably so, because a reasonable person would not have been so provoked or even if provoked, would have cooled off may be found guilty of second degree murder for even though, he intended to kill, his actions lack the afore-thought and deliberation requirement for first-degree murder; and (c) one who, although is reasonably provoked and although a reasonable person would not have cooled off, either is not provoked or actually cools-off kills with time and capacity to premeditate and deliberate is actions, may be guilty of murder in the first-degree.[21]

---

[20] Wayne R. LaFave, *Criminal Law; hornbook series, 4th edition P. 787-788 (2003)* ref: *In re- Fraley, 3 Okla. Crim. 719, 109 P. 295 (1910)* {'If in fact, the defendant's passion did cool, which may be shown by circumstances, such as the transaction of other business in the meantime, rational conversations upon other subjects, evidence of preparation for the killing, etc.' then it is not necessary to inquire as to cooling time, for the homicide is murder when actually done in cold blood}.

[21] *People v. Gingell, (1971), supra at P.70*

MULLANEY V. WILBUR

United State Supreme Court
421 U.S. 684, 95 S.Ct. 1881, 44 L.Ed.2d 508 (1975)

In Maine, to have a murder charge reduced to manslaughter, one charged must establish that he committed the homicide, while in the heat of passion. In *Mullaney v. Wilbur*, the court was asked to decide whether the rule was in accord with the due process mandates, stated *in re Winship, 397 U.S. 358, 364 (1970)*, where the prosecution must prove beyond a reasonable doubt all facts to constitute the crime charged.

The defendant, Still E. Wilbur, Jr., was found guilty of murder, for his fatal attack on Claude Hebert in the latter's hotel room. Wilbur claimed that he attacked Hebert in the heat of passion, as a result of Hebert's homosexual advance on him. In his defense, Wilbur stated that, he lacked the intent to kill and therefore, that the charge be reduced to manslaughter and not murder.

In its decision to affirm the District Court's ruling, the Supreme Court, stated that, an invasion of Constitutional Due process is a Federal issue and that Due Process Clause, demands the prosecution to prove beyond a reasonable doubt the presence of malice, while the defendant must establish he acted in the heat of passion, in a homicide case to comport with the rule in *Winship*.

Note: Find the case for the entire case background and court's opinion to help you answer the questions below.

QUESTIONS

[1] Can the decision to mitigate a defendant's crime from murder to manslaughter be seen as aiding one who kills while in a passion on sudden provocation? What do you think is the rationale behind the crime of voluntary manslaughter? Should such a mitigating factor be extended to defendants who are reasonably provoked to steal for example, or kill their victim during the commission of a crime?

[2] Generally deaths occurring during the commission of a crime (felony) are prosecuted as murder and not manslaughter. Consider a scenario where the defendant involved in a felony had

no intent to kill but death occurred as a result of provocation by the victim. Should defendant's crime be mitigated as manslaughter due to lack of intent to kill? If not, what is the rationale behind prosecuting such crimes as murder?

[3] Consider the argument that the heat of passion defendant is less culpable than any other murder defendant. What is the justification for such conclusion, when there is similar compelling evidence for prosecuting the defendants in both instances of murder? How do you respond to those who say murder is murder, irrespective of the presence of provocation? Detail your answers with analysis in the space provided below.

Notes:

Notes:

Notes: Carefully read the facts below and answer the question choosing the correct one from the multiple choices provided. Please explain the reason for your answer below.

Tim was driving home from work when he noticed his girlfriend Jane, holding hands with Peter a neighborhood playboy. Infuriated, he went to Jane's home and when he saw Peter chatting with her over coffee in the kitchen, he decided it was time to scare the hell out of him. He drew a gun and fired from a distance hitting the coffee mug Peter was drinking from.

The bullet struck and killed Peter. What is the most serious crime Tim has committed?

    (A) First degree murder
    (B) Second degree murder
    (C) Voluntary manslaughter
    (D) Involuntary manslaughter.

Phillip was a Marine who had been experiencing some marital issues with his wife Briana. One night, Phillip came home unannounced from his deployment and found Jack in bed with Briana. Phillip was so angry and disappointed but told Jack to dress up quickly and leave his house. Jack carried a gun in his pocket and thought this might be the opportunity to have Briana to him alone, while he was putting on his pants he reached in his pocket and pulled out his gun. Phillip saw Jack pull out a gun and scared for his life, he quickly pulled out his own military issued revolver and fired a shot killing Jack.

Based on stated facts, Phillip is guilty of

    (A) Voluntary manslaughter
    (B) First degree murder
    (C) Involuntary manslaughter
    (D) Felony murder
    (E) No crime

If Phillip is found not guilty, what best argument below supports the jury's decision?

(A) Phillip has the right to kill when he found another man in his bed
(B) Phillip has the defense of others since Jack was in his bed sleeping with his wife
(C) Jack caused death on himself by entering Phillip's house unauthorized
(D) Phillip has the right to use reasonable deadly force because he was threatened with deadly force by Jack
(E) Phillip has the right to kill any invader irrespective of the circumstances

Mariano and Alonzo decided to kill Jose for testifying against them in a robbery that led to their conviction eight years ago. They met in a bar close to Mariano's house and agreed that Alonzo should carry out the killing. Both injected some cocaine to build courage, while they carried out their plan without mercy. Alonzo took his gun and went to the local post office where Jose worked, while Mariano stayed home waiting for the good news. Minutes after Alonzo left, Mariano had a change of heart and decided to withdraw from the plan because killing Jose, means he could be back in jail if caught. He tried to reach Alonzo to stop him from carrying out the plan but failed. Not long after, Alonzo arrived and indicated "Jose is now cold dead."

If Mariano is prosecuted for conspiracy to commit murder, the fact that he had a change of heart and attempted to withdraw means that:

(A) He was not guilty as charged because he had no hand in the shooting
(B) Still guilty of conspiracy though not vicariously liable for Jose's death
(C) Still guilty because he did not do more to end the plan
(D) Not guilty because he tried to reach Alonzo but failed
(E) Guilty, his withdrawal had no effect because it was never communicated to Alonzo

Notes:

36

PEOPLE V. WASHINGTON

Court of Appeals, Second District
58 Cal.App.3d 620, 130 Cal.Rptr. 96 (1976)

In a trial by jury, the defendant in this case was convicted of murder for violating Penal Code section 187, which was found to be in the second degree. Allegation of the use of a firearm was also found to be true. He was sentenced to state prison and later he decided to appeal judgment.

Based on facts, the victim Owen Wilson Brady was shot and killed by his homosexual partner Merle Francis Washington on August 10, 1974, while the two were riding in the victim's car. The killing was the result of a lover's quarrel, provoked by unfaithfulness on the part of the victim and his expressed desire to terminate the relationship.

On appeal it was raised that because of instructional error and inadequacy of defense trial counsel, the conviction should either be reversed or reduced to voluntary manslaughter by the court.

It is next suggested that, in defining "heat of passion" necessary to reduce murder to manslaughter in a case involving a homosexual, it is error to use the standard of "an ordinary reasonable person of average disposition" but rather should be tested by a standard applicable to a female or to the average servient homosexual.

The jury was instructed that to reduce the homicide from murder to manslaughter upon the ground of sudden quarrel or heat of passion, the conduct must be tested by the ordinarily reasonable man test. Defendant argues without precedent that to so instruct was error because "Homosexuals are not at present a curiosity or a rare commodity. They are a distinct third sexual class between that of male and female, are present in almost every field of endeavor, and are fast achieving a guarded recognition not formerly accorded them. The heat of their passions in dealing with one another should not be tested by standards applicable to the average man or the average woman, since they are aberrant hybrids, with an obvious diminished capacity.

Defendant claimed that since evidence revealed he was acting as a servient homosexual during the period of his relationship with the victim, that his heat of passion should have been tested, either by a standard applicable to a female, or a standard applicable to the average homosexual, and that it was prejudicial error to instruct the jury to determine his heat of passion defense by standard applicable to the average male." The court disagreed, with reference to *Bridgehouse* …[22]

Quoting *people v. Morse, 70 Cal.2d 711 734-735*… the court stated that the test applied in *Bridgehouse*, supra, was applied, to show that "the evidence of defendant's extraordinary character and environmental deficiencies was manifestly irrelevant to the inquiry." In *People v. Logan, 175 Cal. 45, 48-49*…

According to the court, no defendant may establish his own standard of conduct and justify or excuse himself because in fact his passions were aroused, unless, the jury believe that the facts and circumstances were enough to arouse the passions of the ordinary reasonable man. While the court agreed that conduct of the defendant must be measured by that of the ordinary reasonable man placed in identical circumstances, the jury must be informed that the exciting cause must be such as would naturally tend to arouse the passion of the ordinary reasonable man.

Since the jury was properly instructed to use the ordinary reasonable man test, the court saw no error and therefore, affirmed the judgment.

Note: Please find the case above to read the entire court opinion.

NOTES

[1] Consider the argument that homosexuals are not at present a curiosity or a rare commodity and as a result, should be subject to a different standard of scrutiny other than that applicable to the average male. Is such argument sound under equal protection of the constitution? Should the extraordinary nature of homosexuals be relevant to how they are judged in such cases? Note that in *People v. Bridgehouse* it was stated: "to be sufficient to reduce a homicide to manslaughter, the heat of passion must be such as would naturally be aroused in the mind of an ordinary, reasonable person, under the given facts and circumstances, or in the mind of a person of ordinary self control."[23] Is it proper to conclude that homosexuality is a deficiency or aberrant behavior that must be considered in deciding what standard of scrutiny to apply in homicide cases? What legal basis support homosexuality as a deficient factor, to afford it a different standard of scrutiny?

---

[22] *People v. Bridgehouse, Cal.2d.406, 413, 303 P.2d 1018, 1022*… it was said: "To be sufficient to reduce a homicide to manslaughter, the heat of passion must be such as would naturally be aroused in the mind of an ordinary, reasonable person, under the given facts and circumstances, or in the mind of a person of ordinary self control."

[23] *People v. Bridgehouse* supra

[2] In most cases, the question of whether or not the defendant did commit the homicide in the heat of passion is a question of fact for the jury to decide based on the circumstances of the case. In *People v. Logan* the court indicated the applicable standard where it made clear that, it is for the jury to decide based on facts and circumstances of the case, if the evidence are enough to lead them to believe that the defendant did commit the crime, or to create a reasonable doubt in their minds as to whether or not he did commit the crime under the heat of passion.

[3] In ***R v. Raney***, *29 Crim. App. 14 (1942)*, a conviction of murder was reduced to manslaughter, and in its reasoning the court reiterated: "To a one-legged man like the appellant, who is dependent on his crutches, it is obvious that a blow to a crutch, whether it is a blow that knocks the crutch away or not, is something very different from mere words. It seems to us that, if the judge had repeated that part of the appellant's evidence, it would have been very proper to do so, because a blow to a one-legged man's crutch might well be regarded by a jury as an act of provocation."[24]

[4] A loss of self control resulting in homicide may be excusable such that the defendant is only guilty of manslaughter rather than murder, if the jury is convinced that based on the circumstances of the case, including the standard of self control expected of the defendant, they are certain that the act was excusable.

[5] See also **Joshua Dressler, *Rethinking Heat of Passion: A Defense in search of a Rationale*, *73 J.Crim.L. Criminology 421, 466-67 (1982)*:** where it was reiterated that "The point of the partial defense should be that if the ordinary law-abiding person would be expected to be in sufficient control of his emotions so as to respond in an inner directed fashion, or to respond externally, but non- violently, then homicidal conduct by the actor may be fairly perceived as an unreasonable response to reasonable anger. This homicidal conduct would not be entitled to any mitigation. If, however, the provocation is so great that the ordinarily law-abiding person would be expected to lose self-control to the extent that he could not help but act violently, yet he would still have sufficient self-control so that he could avoid using force likely to cause death or great bodily harm in response to the provocation, then we are saying that the actor's moral blameworthiness is found not in his violent response, but in his homicidal violent response. He did not control himself as much as he should have, or as much as common experience tells us he could have, nor as much as the ordinarily law-abiding person would have. Thus, his choice-capabilities were partially undermined by severe and understandable, non-blameworthy anger, but he was not sufficiently

---

[24] *R. v. Raney, 29 Crim. App. 14 (1942)*

in control of his actions so as to merit total acquittal. It is in this case that the traditional defense should apply."

Considering the above statement, should the "ordinary human nature" be set as a standard for determining whether such a case deserves mitigation from first-degree murder to manslaughter? What is reasonable anger when based on all evidence, the actor would not have been provoked to act the way he did but for the victim's action?

[6] Note that sometimes the homicide may be perceived as unreasonable response to a reasonable anger. How best can one determine the reasonableness of the defendant's action? Is this a question for the judge or the jury and why is such standard crucial as a mitigating factor in homicide cases?

[7] Is it sound argument to conclude that in deciding whether to mitigate a first degree homicide to manslaughter, the jury must focus upon the defendant's total life experience in relation to the victim, and attempt to understand in emotional as well as cognitive terms, the defendant's feelings towards the victim? See **State v. Hoyt**, *21 Wis.2d 284 (1964);* is it proper to base the objects of inquiry on the defendant's state of mind immediately before the homicide and the victim's conduct at the exact moment?

PEOPLE V. BERRY

Supreme Court of California, 1976
18 Cal.3d 509, 134 Cal.Rptr. 415, 556 P.2d 777

Defendant Albert Joseph Berry was charged by indictment with one count of murder and one count of assault by means of force likely to produce great bodily injury. ... The indictment was amended to allege one prior felony conviction which defendant admitted. The assault was allegedly committed on July 23, 1974, and the murder on July 26, 1974. In each count, the alleged victim was defendant's wife, Rachel Pessah Berry. A jury found defendant guilty as charged and determined that the murder was of the first degree. Defendant was sentenced to state prison for the term prescribed by law. He appeals from the judgment of conviction.

Defendant contends that there is sufficient evidence in the record to show that he committed the homicide while in a state of uncontrollable rage caused by provocation and flowing from a condition of diminished capacity and therefore that it was error for the trial court to fail to instruct the jury on voluntary manslaughter as indeed he had requested. He claims: (1) that he was entitled to an instruction on voluntary manslaughter as defined by statute (§ 192) since the killing was done upon a sudden quarrel or heat of passion; and (2) that he was also entitled to an instruction on voluntary manslaughter in the context of a diminished capacity defense. ...

In its decision to overturn the conviction, the court cited evidence of a two-week period of provocatory conduct by defendant's wife Rachel, that could arouse a passion of jealousy, pain and sexual rage in an ordinary man of average disposition such as to cause him to act rashly from this passion. Further testimony also revealed that defendant was in the heat of passion under an uncontrollable rage when he killed Rachel.

Therefore, the court concluded that the jury's determination that defendant was guilty of murder of the first degree under the instructions given did not necessarily indicate that, "the factual question posed by the omitted instruction was necessarily resolved adversely to the defendant under other, properly given instructions."... Meaning that the jury had found that defendant had not killed Rachel under a heat of passion. Since this theory of provocation constituted defendant's entire defense to the first count, the court decided that the failure to give such instruction was prejudicial error (*People v. Watson (1956) 46 Cal.2d 818, 836[299 P.2d 243]*), which requires a reversal of conviction of murder of the first degree.[25] ...

Note: Find the case People v. Berry to read the entire case history and opinion of the court. Answer the questions below based on your research.

NOTES AND QUESTIONS

[1] Note that in reaching its decision, the court referenced *Valentine* stating there is no specific type of provocation required by section 192, and that verbal provocation may be sufficient. But sometimes words of insulting and scandalous nature may not be sufficient to incite provocation however, "words conveying information of a fact which constitutes adequate provocation when the fact is observed would constitute adequate provocation."[26] Based on these opinions, should mere insulting words be adequate provocation to mitigate intentional killing to voluntary manslaughter? What level of insulting words are adequate provocation and should such words be accompanied by other physical acts for the killing to qualify for a lesser charge of voluntary manslaughter? See *People v. Pouncey, 437 Mich. 382 (1991)*.

[2] In *Commonwealth v. Pierce, 419 Mass. 28 (1994)*, the court upheld trial court's decision not to instruct on voluntary manslaughter. On September 28, 1988 the defendant and two of his friends, Joshua and John went to David's apartment where they partied, drank whiskey and watched pornographic films. When his friends left briefly to buy cigarettes, David made a sexual gesture at defendant, grabbed his testicles and said, "you know you want it," defendant pushed David away, threw a few kicks, and choked David resulting in his death.[27]

[3] Considering the court's decision in *Commonwealth v. Pierce*, what do you think is the motivating factor in refusing to mitigate the killing to manslaughter? How does *Pierce* differ

---

[25] FN 4. The trial court gave an instruction to the effect that malice is implied when the killing is a direct result of the perpetration of a felony inherently dangerous to human life. Since the only possible felony involved was the assault, which culminated in the strangling, it was error as conceded by the Attorney General, for the court to so instruct. (*People v. Ireland 70 Cal.2d 522, 539-540 (1969)*)

[26] See *Commonwealth v. Berry, 461 Pa. 233, 336 A.2d 262 (1975)*. Where the court reiterated it was error to instruct the jury that there would be sufficient provocation only if defendant actually witnessed the assault of his mother instead of being told of it by her immediately after the culmination of the attack. According to the court there can be sufficient provocation upon a threat or immediate infliction of serious injury upon ones parent, spouse or child based on relationship of the parties and shared concern of one for the well being of the other. In such cases, the killing may be reduced to voluntary manslaughter.

[27] In upholding the trial judge's decision the court held: "Although the gesture was perhaps offensive, it was not the type of behavior that would provoke a reasonable person into a homicidal response."

from *Mullaney v. Wilbur*, where the court did instruct on manslaughter? Remember that just as in *Pierce*, a sexual gesture resulted in a homicide in *Mullaney*.

[4] In *State v. Madden, 61 N.J. 377, 294 A.2d 609 (1972)*, a police officer assigned to an area with racial tension was mobbed and killed when the officer attempted to arrest defendant's friend Williams but injuring him instead. Defendant was convicted of murder even though, the jury was instructed on a manslaughter charge, the defendant contend that the jury should have been informed: (1) that racial or like antagonism or grievances may constitute provocation, and may so serve whether or not the officer was acting in the execution of his duty; and (2) that the illegal arrest of Williams or the shooting could constitute a provocation of bystanders. The court responded: "The first proposition is frivolous, it is no more than this: that racial, ethnic, religious, economic, political, or like grievances within our social order should be deemed sufficient to provoke a member of one group to kill a member of a group he deems opposed to him, or to kill every police officer as a symbol of the social order within which such grievances exist. The proposition is foreign to the subject of voluntary manslaughter. ...[28]

[5] In *State v. Butler, 277 S.C. 452, 290 S.E.2d 1 (1982)*, defendant invited a young lady for a ride and on arrival to a secluded area, she seduced him, redressed herself and indicated she would "cry rape" so as to have an excuse for arriving home late. Defendant panicked and shot her. Based on the facts, the court held defendant was not entitled to a manslaughter instruction. Considering this ruling, should the court have allowed the instruction if facts show that defendant was indeed afraid of the possibility of a conviction for a crime he did not commit and for which he may be charged; in this case, rape? What about the argument that had defendant allowed the victim to "cry rape" rather than shoot her, facts would have revealed defendant was innocent. How logical is such argument? And does this explain why refusal of manslaughter instruction may be proper? In other words, would the instruction have been proper if the provocation is both actual and reasonable? Please explain the meaning of *actual* and *reasonable* provocation in your response.

---

[28] As to the second proposition, the court assumed that the shooting of Williams involved use of excessive force however, provocation should be disallowed in such circumstances for two reasons: (1) "we believe a man of ordinary firmness would not be provoked to a deadly attack and (2) that the protection a police officer should have in the public interest might be diluted if his mistaken use of force were accepted as an affront to a bystander."

[6] Sometimes an instruction may be given where it is not needed or where the defendant has not requested for one. If the charge is mitigated and defendant is convicted of a lesser crime of manslaughter rather than murder, defendant may appeal based on the argument that it was error to instruct on manslaughter and that without such instruction, he would have been acquitted.[29]

---

[29] *Elmore v. Commonwealth, 520 S.W.2d 328 KY (1975)* Where a manslaughter conviction reversed since instruction was improper and was not requested by defendant; there is no evidence that defendant (Taylor) met his death; ... "In a sudden affray or a sudden heat of passion."

Notes:

Notes: Read the following facts and select the answer from the choices provided.

Holt a neighborhood gang member was in a bar with some of his friends when he saw Ben entering from a distance with Carmen his best friend. Ben is gay and since he came out, Holt has been embarrassing him and calling him a "girly boy," in front of everybody. On several occasions, Ben told Holt to stop the jokes but the taunting became worse and Ben could not take it anymore. Holt walked over to Ben, he offered a handshake and said "Waz up girly boy." When Ben refused to accept his handshake he went over to Carmen and said sarcastically, "Why don't you get yourself a real man like me instead of a girly boy." Unable to take the abuse anymore, ben picked a broken vase of glass in a trash and lunged at Holt attempting to stab him in the chest. Fearing for his life, Holt pushed Ben backward. The force caused Ben to trip and hit his head against a pillar holding the bar. Ben became unconscious and died on the spot few minutes later.

Holt has been charged with murder and you are his attorney. Explain how you intend to defend him in this case. Do you think your client is guilty of any crime? Does it matter that Holt provoked the attack?

Based on the facts as stated above, the most serious offense with which Holt may be properly convicted is:

(A) **Felony murder**

(B) **Involuntary manslaughter**

(C) **Voluntary manslaughter**

(D) **Depraved heart murder**

(E) **Negligence homicide**

(F) **None of the above**

Imagine that Holt is found not guilty of any crime. Which of the following arguments best support his case:

(A) **Holt provoked Ben's action but he did not attack first**

(B) **Ben was the initial aggressor and therefore deserved what he got**

(C) **Holt is entitled to use the amount of force that he used against Ben in self-defense**

(D) **Holt was threatened with a death or serious bodily injury and therefore, need not retreat but use the force reasonably necessary in self-defense**

(E) **(C) And (D) above**

(F) **None of the above**

Janet and Carl his millionaire husband have been married for more than twelve years. Carl made his millions before the marriage but because he loved Janet so much, he decided to put her in-charge of his money and the accounting. Janet also had the privilege of writing checks and making payment for all company expenses. For the past one-year, Carl received several letters indicating he owed the IRS $2 million dollars in back taxes. Janet has been stealing from the company accounts and had diverted all tax money to a private account she kept. She kept all letters from the IRS and never informed Carl about the back taxes. Knowing Carl was about to find out, Janet hired Roscoe a professional assassin and paid him $2,000 to kill Carl. Roscoe took the money and killed Carl.

You are the attorney hired by Carl's family to make sure Janet is found guilty and put behind bars. How will you argue your case against the defense and what are the charges you will put forward? Discuss your answer in a two-page essay below.

If Janet is arrested and she confesses to stealing the company's money, she can be charged with theft and:

(A) Murder only

(B) Conspiracy only

(C) Conspiracy or murder, but not both

(D) Conspiracy and murder

(E) Only theft because Roscoe killed Carl not Janet

Imagine that Janet is convicted of theft, conspiracy and murder, which of the followings is likely to help the jury reach a verdict:

(A) Janet had no contract with Roscoe but paid Roscoe for the killing

(B) Janet entered into an agreement with Roscoe to commit an illegal act

(C) Roscoe a co-conspirator committed a crime in furtherance of the conspiracy therefore, Janet is equally guilty

(D) Janet can be convicted of theft, conspiracy and murder because conspiracy liability, will not merge into the completed crime

(E) (B), (C) And (D) above

Notes:

Notes: Consider the scenario below and choose your answer from the choices provided. Analyze the facts in the question and explain why your choice is right in the space given.

Officer received a call via 911 that Daniel the 14-year-old, neighborhood bully was brandishing a gun and scaring people in the park. Officer responded to the call and on arrival at the park saw Daniel reaching for the gun. Without warning, Officer opened fire and killed Daniel instantly. Investigation later revealed it was a toy gun.

Is Officer guilty of Murder?

   (A) Yes, because Officer did not warn Daniel
   (B) Yes, because Officer intended to kill Daniel
   (C) No, because Officer believed he was in danger
   (D) No, if Officer reasonably believed his life was in danger

If not murder, what crime do you think Officer can reasonably be charged with? Explain all your answers below.

Notes:

Chapter Four

Homicide By Premeditation

At common law, only one form of murder was recognized and all murders were punished equally, the murderer was executed. However, in the current system and age, judges realized that the common law rule was harsh and that not all homicides should be punished equally. The result is that, homicides were divided into murder and manslaughter with manslaughter punishable by incarceration, rather than death. Murder as defined by common law was: (1) The unlawful killing of a (2) human being with (3) malice aforethought. The requirement of malice aforethought helped distinguished murder from manslaughter, a lesser charge.

Although the requirement of malice aforethought is stated differently by the States, under the common law rule of homicide, the following became recognized as murder: (1) When it is established the defendant charged, intended to cause the death of the victim; (2) When the defendant intended to cause serious bodily harm, resulting in death; (3) When the defendant created an unreasonably high risk of death, which indeed caused the victim's death, irrespective of defendant's intent otherwise, known as "depraved –heart murder" and finally; (4) Wherever felony murder was applicable.

As indicated in earlier chapters, most jurisdictions today have done away with the common law homicide rule and have recognized degrees of murder. Few of the States still depend on the common law definition of malice aforethought but nonetheless, many still subscribe to the felony-murder doctrine. First-degree murder is the highest form of murder, which is why it is severely punished more than second-degree murder and other degrees of murder including manslaughter.

To be of the first degree, it must be shown that the homicide was *willful*, *deliberate*, and *premeditated*. 'Generally, it is first- degree murder whenever the murderer has as a goal the death of the victim. *Willful*, as used in first-degree murder, is a specific intent concept. To be *willful*, the defendant must have specifically intended to cause the death. *Deliberate* is usually defined as a cool mind, not acting out of an immediate passion, fear, or rage. The term *premeditation* means to think before hand and similar to d*eliberate*, it eliminates impulsive acts from the grasp of first-degree murder'.[30]

---

[30] Daniel E. Hall, *Survey of Criminal Law*: Second Edition, (1997) p.98.

STATE V. GUTHRIE

Supreme Court of Appeals of West Virginia
194 W. Va. 657, 461 S.E.2d 163 (1995)

Dale Edward Guthrie, the defendant in this case, appeals a January 1994, jury verdict of the Circuit Court of Kanawha County finding him guilty of first-degree murder. In May of 1994, he was sentenced to serve a life sentence with a recommendation of mercy.

On the evening of February 12, 1993, the defendant took a knife from his pocket and stabbed his co-worker, Steven Todd Farley, in the neck and killed him. Both men worked together as dishwashers at Danny's Rib House in Nitro and got along well with each other before this incident. On the night of the killing, the victim, his brother, Tracy Farley, and James Gibson were joking around while working in the kitchen of the restaurant. The victim was poking fun at the defendant who appeared to be in a bad mood. He told the defendant to "lighten up" and snapped him with a dishtowel several times. Apparently, the victim had no inkling he was upsetting the defendant very much. The dishtowel flipped the defendant on the nose and he became enraged. The defendant removed his gloves and started toward the victim, Mr. Farley, still teasing said: "Ooo, he's taking his gloves off." The defendant then pulled a knife from his pocket and stabbed the victim in the neck. He also stabbed Mr. Farley in the arm as he fell to the floor. Mr. Farley looked up and cried: "Man, I was just kidding around." The defendant responded: "Well man, you should have never hit me in my face." On arrival of the police, the defendant said he killed the victim and he was arrested. Evidence showed that prior to the incident, the defendant suffers from a host of psychiatric problems, depression (dysthymic disorder), an obsession with his nose (body dysmorphic disorder), and borderline personality disorder...

The State claimed that the facts supported a first-degree murder conviction. At the close of the State's case-in-chief, the defense moved for a directed verdict contending the State failed to present evidence of malice and premeditation. The motion was denied. The defense argued the facts of the case supported voluntary manslaughter or at worse, second degree murder. The jury returned a verdict finding the defendant guilty of first-degree murder with a recommendation of mercy. ...

The court stated that, to find defendant guilty of first degree murder, the jury must have believed that: (1) the "horseplay" provocation was not sufficient to justify a deadly attack; (2) the defendant was under no real fear of his own from being attacked; (3) the stabbing was intentional; and (4) the time it took the defendant to open his knife and inflict the mortal wound was sufficient to establish premeditation.[31]

According to the court, to establish deliberate and premeditated killing, it is not necessary that the intention to kill should exist for any particular length of time prior to the actual killing it is only necessary that such intention should have come into existence for the first time at the time of such killing or at any time previously.

While the court agreed that temperaments of people differ according to the circumstances in which they may be placed, it also believed that any interval of time between the forming of the intent to kill and the execution of that intent, which is of sufficient duration for the accused to be fully conscious of what he intended, is sufficient to support a conviction for first degree murder.

In conclusion, the court approved a new instruction in the area of homicide law, but said it did not believe its decision should be applied retroactively. The case was remanded, giving defendant the benefit of the decision on remand. …

Note: Locate the entire case history and court opinion from a reliable source. Answer the following questions based on your findings.

NOTES AND QUESTIONS

[1] Considering the majority opinion in *Guthrie*, is it proper to conclude that based on the language of the opinion, the majority is of the view that some appreciable length of time must pass before premeditation is established?

[2] At trial, every element[32] of a crime must be proven beyond a reasonable doubt (criminal cases) by the prosecution. For example, if an element of a crime is missing and not proven beyond a reasonable doubt, the defendant walks and may not be found guilty. The rule is that each element

---

[31] Based on evidence, the defendant became irritated by victim's action before the stabbing. His anger was building with each comment and flip of the towel by the victim; according to witnesses defendant attempted to stab the victim the second time as he fell to the ground but slashing him in the arm instead and finally, the defendant's indication that he "had the right to respond, finally, to this act of aggression that was perpetrated against him" is considered probative evidence of premeditation and deliberation.

[32] **Element:** This is a component of a crime, all crimes have elements stated in the law and that must be proven before conviction can be found; the element represents an essential part of the proscribed offense that must be used as guide in determining whether the defendant committed the crime.

must be proved individually. If a crime consists of four elements, all four must be proven beyond reasonable doubt in order to find the defendant guilty of the crime. If three of the elements have been proven and one is not then, there must be a not guilty verdict. This rule is true even when the jury is absolutely convinced that all the other elements were true and that the defendant committed the crime. Why do you think such a strict rule of criminal justice is subscribed to by most jurisdictions? Some have argued that human life is so valuable and in order to find one guilty of a crime and sentence for the crime, all elements of the crime must be established. Should courts continue to adhere to such rule when all evidence show the defendant did commit the crime even though, the prosecution by error may have failed to prove one element of the crime? How applicable is such strict rule to the *O.J. Simpson* and the *Casey Anthony* case?

[3] In most cases, if one crime has been proven, all the elements of a related lesser crime can also be proved. A defendant convicted of killing a person with a baseball bat, has also committed a battery of the victim but in such situations, the *merger doctrine*[33] takes effect and the lesser crime merges into the greater offense. In applying *merger*, both crimes may be charged however, if the defendant is convicted of the greater offense, the lesser crime is absorbed by the greater, and the defendant is not punished for both as this will amount to *double jeopardy* that is, punishing the defendant twice for the same criminal act.

[4] Consider the argument that," if intent is deliberate and premeditated whenever there is choice, then in truth it is always deliberate and premeditated, since choice is involved in the hypothesis of the intent."[34] Based on such argument, should the court have found the defendant in *Guthrie* guilty of a lesser crime? Do you think that the suddenness of the intent and the passion involved as a result of provocation by the victim are enough for the jury to exercise mercy?

In *People v. Smithey, 20 Cal.4th 936, 86 Cal.Rptr.2d 243, 978 P.2d 1171 (1999)*, the following instruction was given: "All murder which is perpetrated by any kind of willful, deliberate and premeditated killing with express malice aforethought is murder of the first degree. The word '*deliberate*' means formed or arrived at or determined upon as a result of the careful thought and weighing and consideration for and against the proposed course of action. The word '*premeditated*' means considered beforehand. If you find that the killing was preceded and accompanied by a clear, deliberate intent on the part of the defendant to kill, which was the result of deliberation

---

[33] **Merger Doctrine:** Under this doctrine, when a lesser offense is a component of a greater offense, the lesser charge merges into the greater charge and the defendant may only be prosecuted for the greater offense.

[34] Wayne R. Lafave, *Modern Criminal Law supra, ref.* **Benjamin Cardozo, Law and Literature and Other Essays and Addresses 99-101 (1931)** at note (1) P. 294.

and premeditation, so it must have been formed upon preexisting reflection and not under a sudden heat of passion or other condition precluding the idea of deliberation, it is murder in the first degree. *To prove the killing was deliberate and premeditated, it shall not be necessary to prove the defendant maturely and meaningfully reflected upon the gravity of this act.* The law does not undertake to measure in units of time the length of the period during which the thought must be pondered before it can ripen into an intent to kill, which is truly deliberate and premeditated. The time will vary with different individual and other varying circumstances. The true test is not the duration of time, but rather the extent of the reflection. A cold, calculated judgment and decision may be arrived at in a short period of time, but a mere unconsidered and rash impulse, even though it include an intent to kill, is not such deliberation and premeditation as will fix an unlawful killing as murder of the first degree. To constitute a deliberate and premeditated killing, the slayer must weigh and consider the question of killing and the reasons for and against such a choice and, having in mind the consequences, he decides to and does kill."

[5] Considering the instruction above, do you see any correlation between such instruction and insanity defenses in first-degree murder cases? Why are such crimes mitigated from first degree to a lesser degree of homicide? Explain your answer by analyzing the instruction above. Is there a link recognized in criminal law between choice and the intent to kill? Check the homicide statute of your jurisdiction to find what makes a killing, murder of the first degree and determine where insanity defenses apply.

[6] Based on the instruction in note [4] above, do you think the court in *Guthrie* reached the right conclusion? Explain.

In ***State v. Snowden, 79 Idaho 266, 313 P.2d 706 (1957)***; Defendant Snowden had been playing pool and drinking in a Boise poolroom early in the evening with a companion, one Carrier, he visited a club near Boise, then, went to a nearby Garden City. There the two men visited a number of bars, and defendant had several drinks. Their last stop was the HiHo club.

Witnesses related that while defendant was in the HiHo Club he met and talked to Cora Lucyle Dean. The defendant himself said he hadn't been acquainted with Mrs. Dean prior to that time, but he had "seen her in a couple of the joints up town." He danced with Mrs. Dean while at the HiHo Club. Upon departing from the tavern, the two left together.

In statements to police officers, that were admitted in evidence, defendant Snowden said after they left the club Mrs. Dean wanted him to find a cab and take her back to Boise, and he refused because he didn't feel he should pay her fare. After some words, he related:

"She got mad at me so I got pretty hot and I don't know whether I back handed her there or not. And, we got calmed down and decided to walk across to the gas station and call a cab."

They crossed the street, and began arguing again. Defendant said: "She swung and at the same time she kneed me again. I blew my top."

Defendant said he pushed the woman over beside a pickup truck, which was standing near a business building. There he pulled his knife a pocket knife with a two-inch blade and cut her throat.

The body, which was found the next morning was viciously and sadistically cut and mutilated. An autopsy surgeon testified the voice box had been cut, and that this would have prevented the victim from making any intelligible cry. There were other wounds inflicted while she was still alive- one in her neck, one in her abdomen, two in the face, and two on the back of the neck. The second neck wound severed the spinal cord and caused her death. There were other wounds all over the body, and her clothing had been cut away. The nipple of her right breast was missing. There was no evidence of sexual attack on the victim; however, some of the lacerations were around the breasts and vagina of the deceased. ***

Murder is defined by statute as follows:

All murder which is perpetrated by means of poison, or lying in wait, torture or by any other kind of willful, deliberate and premeditated killing, or which is committed in the perpetration of, or attempt to perpetrate arson, rape, robbery, burglary, kidnapping, or mayhem is murder in the first degree. All other murders are of the second degree.

The defendant admitted taking the life of the deceased.

The principal argument of the defendant pertaining to [the charge of premeditated murder] is that the defendant did not have sufficient time to develop a desire to take the life of the victim but rather his action was instantaneous and a normal reaction to the physical injury which she dealt him. ***

There need be no appreciable space of time between the intention to kill and the act of killing. They may be as instantaneous as successive thoughts of the mind. It is only necessary that the act of killing be preceded by a concurrence of will, deliberation and premeditation on the part of the slayer, and, if such is the case, the killing is murder in the first degree.

In the present case, the trial court had no other alternative than to find the defendant guilty of willful, deliberate, and premeditated killing with malice aforethought in view of the defendant's acts in deliberately opening up a pocket knife, next cutting the victim's throat, and then hacking and cutting until he had killed Cora Lucyle Dean. ***

QUESTIONS

[1] Assume that the defendant in *Snowden* lacked the specific intent to kill or commit premeditated murder, do you think he should have been found guilty of a lesser degree of murder, considering the gravity of wound inflicted on the victim? Does the nature and extent of wound on the victim matter?

Notes:

[2] *Akinloye* saw his live-in girlfriend *Lola* riding in the car with another man, he approached her and said "better not come home tonight or you are dead." *Lola* feels threatened and decides to go stay at her mom's. The following day she was found dead with four stab wounds to the chest and her vagina area badly mutilated. Traces of blood found at the scene turned out to be *Akinloye's* and the DNA found at the scene also a match however, nobody saw *Akinloye* commit the crime but evidence revealed he was not home at the time of the murder though, was later seen at a bar near the victim's house. What crime if any is *Akinloye* guilty of? Do you consider this a crime of passion? If so, why? If not explain. Assuming the defendant is found guilty of first-degree murder, does the defendant have any chance of mitigating the charge to a lesser one? Please explain below why or why not with reference to *Snowden*.

Notes:

[3] The fully clothed body of Mrs. Mesa was found in her home, where she had bled to death from 38 knife wounds to the head, face, neck, back, and arms, none to a vital organ. Two different knives had been used, including the one found broken under her body. There were blood drops throughout the master bedroom, and drops of blood were found inside jewelry boxes and on clothing inside open drawers. In the kitchen, many of the cupboards and drawers were open, and drops of blood were found inside some drawers, including one containing knives. Mr. Mesa found nothing missing from the house except one of his dress shirts. Defendant, who had attended high school with Mrs. Mesa and her husband, was charged with the murder when his fingerprints were found in the house, his father produced the missing shirt, defendant was found to have a cut on his hand, and defendant's blood matched that found about the Mesa's house.[35] Based on the following evidence, may the defendant be found guilty of first-degree murder? In your answer, please refer to *State v. Guthrie* and base your analysis on the *Anderson* formula. Do you think the circumstances surrounding Mrs. Mesa's death is enough to find defendant guilty of first degree murder, if at all? In your answer, consider the familiarity and the relationship between defendant and Mrs. Mesa. Do you think such a relationship indicate a motive to commit murder? Give your answers below and explain as if in a courtroom prosecuting the case.

·

---

[35] *People v. Perez, 2 Cal. 4ᵗʰ 1117, 9 Cal. Rptr.2d 577(1992)* in which, it was held the evidence sufficient under the *Anderson* method for determining when first-degree murder conviction is proper. Refer to *State v. Guthrie supra,* for the discussion.

[4] Think about the nature and manner of death of Mrs. Mesa; is there any indication of a deliberate intention to kill? Or any proof of a preconceived design to commit a homicide? Please explain your answers with references to two other relevant cases of murder you know. How does this case compare to *Snowden* above?

Notes:

Notes: Please discuss below any defenses you think the defendant above may have if any at all.

Chapter Five
Negligent Homicide

Intent to Do Serious Bodily Harm and the Deadly Weapon Doctrine

One way of mitigating a murder from first degree to a lesser degree is by showing the defendant had no intent or design to kill however, the defendant only intended to cause a serious bodily harm to the victim. Where facts indicate the defendant intended something less than a serious bodily harm to the victim, the crime may be mitigated as manslaughter, which may be a form of negligent or reckless homicide.

In certain situations, the jury acting as the finder of fact may look at the evidence to determine the state of mind of the defendant at the time of the offense. Based on such determination, the jury may conclude the defendant intended death and as a result, convict him of murder in the first degree. However, if based on evidence it is clear the defendant did not intend death, but rather did intend to inflict serious bodily injury on the victim, then the crime may be of second-degree murder.

Under the *deadly weapon doctrine*, the jury may infer the defendant intended to kill his victim, if a *deadly weapon* was used to commit the offense. However, this is for the fact finder to determine and such conclusion does not have to be drawn. For example, if *Akin* intended to only injure *wale* by stabbing him with a knife and in the process *wale* died from his wounds, the jury may convict *Akin* of first-degree murder. However, the jury may not draw such conclusion if based on facts, it is determined *Akin* only intended to inflict serious bodily injury on *wale* and not kill him then, in such case *Akin* may face a second degree murder charge or manslaughter.

Under the *deadly weapon doctrine*, any device may be termed a deadly weapon if, based on the manner of use it is likely to produce death or serious bodily injury. For example, a fist meant to inflict a fatal blow on the victim, may be a deadly weapon if the manner of use is know to be capable of causing death. A fatal blow from a professional boxer is considered a deadly weapon, when used on a non-professional. Under the Model Penal Code a deadly weapon is "any firearm, or other weapon, device, instrument, material, or substance, whether animate or inanimate, which in the manner it is used or is intended to be used, is known to be capable of producing death or serious bodily injury."[36]

Under the Model Penal Code, some items that are not in normal daily usage considered deadly may become deadly weapon if their use is intended to inflict serious bodily injury to the victim or death. Also, other items which are considered deadly may not be, if based on use it poses no threat of serious injury or death to the victim. For example, a metal chair, which normally is designed for sitting when used for its purpose, may become a deadly weapon if used to crush the victim's head. Likewise, a gun considered a deadly weapon when used to shoot a person, may not be a deadly weapon if only used to hit the victim over the head.

---

[36] Daniel E. Hall, *Survey of Criminal Law supra: ref.* Model Penal Code, P. 102

STATE V. HARDIE

Supreme Court of Iowa, 1878
47 Iowa 647

In this case the defendant was a boarder in the family of one Gantz, his brother in-law. Mrs. Sutfen, a neighbor, came to the house, and after some friendly conversation she went into the kitchen. When she came back defendant picked up a tack hammer and struck on the door. She said, "My God, I thought it was a revolver." A short time afterwards she went into the yard to get a kitten. Defendant said he would frighten her with the revolver as she came in. He took a revolver from a stand drawer and went out of the room, and was in the kitchen when the revolver was discharged. He immediately came in and said to Mrs. Gantz, his sister, "My God, Hannah, come and see what I have done." His sister went out and found Mrs. Sutfen lying on the sidewalk at the side of the house, with a gunshot wound in the head, and in a dying condition. After a physician examination in which it became clear nothing could be done for the deceased, the defendant became violent, said the shot was accidental, and exclaimed several times that he would kill himself. He was later restrained to prevent him from harming himself.

The revolver had been in the house for about five years. Gantz found it in the road. It had just one load in it when found. Six months after it was found Gantz tried to shoot the load from it but was unsuccessful. He tried to punch the load out, but could not move it. He then put it away with the impression that it was harmless. The defendant lived in the house and knew the condition of the revolver. Upon one occasion Gantz said he would try to kill a cat with the revolver. Defendant there at the time, said he would not be afraid to allow it to be snapped at him all day. The revolver remained in the same condition that it was when found, no other load having been put into it, and it was considered by the family as well as defendant as entirely harmless.

The State claimed that the defendant was guilty of manslaughter because of criminal carelessness. The defendant insisted that there was no such carelessness as to render the act criminal, and that it was homicide by misadventure, and therefore excusable.

The court instructed the jury that if the defendant used a dangerous and deadly weapon, in a careless and reckless manner, and as a result he killed the deceased, then he is guilty of manslaughter, although he meant no harm.

On the issue of criminal carelessness, the court instructed the jury that, if the death of the party was a result of recklessness and carelessness of the defendant then he should be convicted, and if not the jury must acquit. According to the instruction, the defendant must be held to the degree of care reasonably prudent man should and ought to use under like circumstances, and if he did not use such care he should be convicted, or else acquitted.

Attorney for defendant rejected the instruction and asked the court to instruct that though, the deceased died from the discharge of a pistol by the defendant, yet if the defendant believed, that the pistol which caused her death was not in any manner dangerous, but entirely harmless, and if he acted like a man of ordinary prudence and caution might have done under like circumstances, then the jury should find him not criminally liable and should acquit.

The court rejected the instruction and in its decision to affirm the conviction for manslaughter, the court based its decision partly on the grossly reckless behavior of the defendant and indicated that, no jury would be warranted in finding that men of ordinary prudence so conduct themselves, since human life is not to be sported with by the use of firearms, even though, the person using them may have good reason to believe that the weapon used is not loaded, or that being loaded it will do no injury. When persons engage in such reckless sport they should be held liable for the consequences of their acts.

In conclusion, the court stated that evidence showing defendant, took the weapon from the drawer with the avowed purpose of frightening the deceased, and while in his hands it was discharged killing victim, together with his confession that he did the act, fully warranted the jury in finding that he purposely pointed the pistol and discharged it at the deceased.

Note: Research the case to read the entire case history and opinion that made the court to affirm the conviction. Locating the case will help you answer the questions.

QUESTIONS

[1] Consider the instruction by the judge that "I do not mean that defendant is to be held to the highest degree of care and prudence in handling a dangerous and deadly weapon, but only such care as a reasonably prudent man should and ought to use under like circumstances." Explain what is meant by this instruction? What does the judge mean by "a reasonably prudent man?"

Notes:

[2] Based on the instruction in question (1) assume the defendant in this case is a retired police officer trained in the use of a gun and the facts as is; do you think the same instruction, should apply? If so, why? Use space below for your answer.

Notes:

[3] Same instruction above, *Ladi* invited his friend *Dale* home for lunch; both friends are of legal age. *Ladi* recalled his dad a retired marine had his revolver locked in his bedroom, in fact, *Ladi* remembered his father told him never to touch the gun that it was loaded for security purposes but locked and would not go off. *Ladi* wanted to show-off his dad's shining revolver, went to his bedroom, took the gun from its container and showed it to his friend at the table. At one point, he pointed the gun at his friend and said, "you can't imagine what this baby can do." *Ladi* placed his finger on the trigger and tried to pull. *Dale* exclaimed "what are you doing, don't point that baby at me it may go off." *Ladi* responded "don't worry it won't go off, my dad locked it." Suddenly, the gun went off and *Dale* was killed with a shot to the head. Based on the facts, what crime if any is Ladi guilty of? Is the same instruction above proper for the defendant in this case? Explain argumentatively below.

Notes:

74

[4] Considering the facts above, is *Ladi*'s dad guilty of any crime? If so, why? If not explain below.

Notes:

[5] In *Commonwealth v. Malone, 354 Pa. 180, 47 A.2d 445 (1946)*, two friends had a revolver, containing one cartridge in the chamber, so positioned that it would not go off until the trigger had been pulled about five times. One playfully put the gun against the side of the other and pulled the trigger three times. At the third pull, the gun went off resulting in a fatal shot. The court affirmed a conviction of second-degree murder.

Notes:

[6] Apply *Malone* to the facts in question (3) above is a conviction for second-degree murder proper for the defendant in question (3)? What differentiates *Malone* and the facts in question (3) as stated? To answer the question, please read *Commonwealth v. Malone* and answer this question as a group assignment. Deliberate among yourselves as a group and come up with a reasonable answer.

In *Hyam v. Director of Public Prosecution (1975) A.C. 55, (1974) 2 W.L.R. 602, (1974) 2 All E.R. 41;* The defendant appeals her conviction after setting a fire that resulted in the death of two girls. The defendant's defense was that she had started the fire only with the intention of frightening Mrs. Booth into leaving the neighborhood, and that she had no intention of death or serious bodily harm. The court reiterated that the presence of an intention to kill or cause grievous bodily harm is what convicts a murderer who takes a very long shot at his victim and kills him regardless of whether he thinks correctly as he takes his aim that the odds are very much against his hitting him at all.

In the field of guilty knowledge it is accepted both for the purposes of criminal and civil law that "a man who deliberately shuts his eyes to the truth will not be heard to say that he did not know it." The same can be said of the state of intention of a man who, with actual appreciation of the risks and without lawful excuse, willfully decides to expose potential victims to the risk of death or really serious injury regardless of whether the consequences take place or not. Since a rational man must be taken to intend the consequences of his acts, it is the man's actual state of knowledge and intent, which, as in all cases determines his criminal responsibility.

[7] Based on the court opinion in *Hyam,* can one conclude that the defendant knew or should have known the gun might go off? If so, how did you reach this conclusion? If not, explain.

Notes:

[8] Do you consider it legally sound to equate the intent to frighten to the intent to cause serious bodily harm? If so, should the defendant in *Hardie* be guilty of murder instead of manslaughter?

Notes:

[9] Is it legally sound to conclude that because the defendant took the weapon from the drawer with the intent to frighten the victim, knowing the victim, had once expressed her fear of being frightened when she said, "My God, I thought it was a revolver," is enough evidence to find defendant guilty of murder and not manslaughter?

Notes:

[10] What role did the legal doctrine of *assumption of the risk* play in finding defendant guilty of manslaughter? Explain with reference to the case and consider the following in note [11].

Notes:

[11] **Model Penal Code** § 210.2 "Since risk … is a matter of degree and the motive for risk creation may be infinite in variation, some formula is needed to identify the case where recklessness may be found and where it should be assimilated to purpose or knowledge for purposes of grading. … In a prosecution for murder, *** the code calls for the further judgment whether the actor's conscious disregard of the risk, under the circumstances, manifests extreme indifference to the value of human life. The significance of purpose or knowledge as a standard of culpability is that, cases of provocation or other mitigation apart, purposeful or knowing homicide demonstrates precisely such indifference to the value of human life. Whether recklessness is so extreme that it demonstrates similar indifference is not a question that can be further clarified. It must be left directly to the trier of fact under instructions." Do you agree? Explain how the Model Penal Code as stated applied to the defendant in *Hardie*.

Notes:

[12] *Kunle* knowing he had a vicious German Shepard allowed the dog to roam the neighborhood unleashed. The dog mauled and killed *Biola* a six-month-old baby as she rode in a stroller.

Is Kunle guilty of murder?

(A) Yes, Kunle is guilty of murder because his dog intended to kill the baby

(B) Yes, because Kunle should have known he had a vicious dog

(C) No, because it was the dog that killed baby not Kunle

(D) No, Kunle is only guilty of negligent homicide for failing to take reasonable care

(E) Kunle is guilty of a lesser crime depending on the circumstances of the case

(F) None of the above.

Notes:

[13] John and Sam decided it would be proper to have an early Halloween though the event was three weeks away. They dressed up as monsters at 2.00am in the morning and proceeded to Ms. Booth's house. They do know her very well, but this time they want to give her the scare of her life. Ms. Booth was sound asleep so, they entered her apartment through the kitchen door in the back of the house, went in her room and screamed "Surprise the monsters are here to devour." Ms. Booth woke up suddenly with extreme fear, suffered a heart attack, and died instantly. Are John and Sam guilty of murder? If so, why? If not what is the possible crime they could be charged with? You must answer the question as an essay in the space provided but before, look at the multiple choices question below.

Same scenario as above but assume that Mrs. Booth is known to have a serious heart problem in fact, she had suffered a heart attack twice. Knowing such fact, are Sam and John guilty of murder?

(A) Yes, because Mrs. Booth's previous heart attacks is irrelevant
(B) Yes, because scaring her triggered her death
(C) No, because her prior heart condition probably killed her
(D) Both are guilty of negligent homicide irrespective of Mrs. Booth's heart issues
(E) None of the above.

Notes:

[14] *Dele* is known to sometimes suffer from seizures, his doctor told him not to drive 4hrs after taking his medication. Just an hour after taking his prescription, he decided to go pick up his check before the office is closed. Though, he was driving carefully, the drug made him dizzy. He lost control of the vehicle and struck a teenager who died instantly. Is *Dele* guilty of murder or manslaughter? What is the least possible crime he could be charged with? Does he have any chance of mitigating the charge such that he only gets a slap on the wrist? That is, he walks. Argue the case in defense of Dele and explain why he should not be guilty of murder or manslaughter in the space provided. Your arguments must be at least a page long.

Apply same scenario as stated above to the following question. Based on the facts, Dele must be guilty of what crime?

(A) **Murder**

(B) **Manslaughter**

(C) **Negligent homicide for failing to take reasonable care despite the medication**

(D) **Dele could be charged with a lesser crime under a vehicular homicide statute**

(E) **Dele walks because the drug not him caused the death of teenager**

(F) **None of the above**

Notes:

[15] *Dayo* was pursued by the highway patrol for driving through the red light and going beyond the speed limit. As she is pursued, she decided to go faster to make sure the police don't beat her to the game. She was going at 120 M.P.H. on a 55 M.P.H limit road. Unbeknownst, a couple returning from the wedding reception was coming in a car and about to cross the lane in front of her. *Dayo* skipped the red light and collided with the other vehicle. The groom and the couple's driver died but the bride survived with serious injuries.

Based on facts, what crime or crimes is Dayo guilty of? Assume that the incident occurred in New York.

(A) **Murder and traffic violation for acting with indifference to life when he took off from highway patrol**

(B) **Murder for assuming the risk that innocent bystanders may end up dead**

(C) **Murder for acting recklessly thereby causing death**

(D) **Guilty of traffic violation and a lesser crime of homicide, because he lacked intent and did not know his action would result in death**

(E) **A, B and C above**

(F) **None of the above**

NOTE

"Four distinct approaches dominate the modern treatment of unintended murder": (1) the objective circumstances approach, which focuses upon the circumstances surrounding the crime rather than the defendant's attitude towards the victim's life, such as with the New York requirement that the jury determine whether the defendant's acts were themselves "brutal, callous, dangerous and inhuman"; (2) the degree of risk approach, which limits murder to cases in which the defendant's acts created a particularly significant chance of causing a death; (3) the multiple victim approach, whereunder a defendant is guilty only if his reckless act endangers more than one individual; and (4) the *mens rea* approach, which requires some state of mind more culpable than recklessness. At section 807 of the note, it was indicated that the latter approach is the best; that in jurisdictions where the approach obtains we "have failed to put the question of indifference to courts and juries in a sufficiently concrete and definite manner"; and that extreme indifference can best be discovered "by asking the finder of fact whether the actor would have committed the act had he known it would cause death."[37]

---

[37] Wayne R. Lafave, *Modern Criminal Law* supra; ref. Model Penal Code § 210.2 note, 85 Colum. L.Rev. 786, 789-90 (1985) at P. 309

STATE V. BIER

Supreme Court of Montana, 1979
181 Mont. 27, 591 P.2d 1115

This is an appeal from a conviction of negligent homicide. In the morning of June 25, 1977, Deputy Sheriff Donovan responded to a call about a possible suicide at the Red Wheel Trailer Court in Great Falls. He arrived at about 1:30 A.M. and met defendant Richard Bier. Donovan entered the trailer and found Sharon Bier, defendant's wife dead on the floor with a neck wound. Defendant told Donovan that his wife shot herself, with A 357 Magnum revolver.

According to defendant, he and his wife had three six-packs of beer. Mrs. Bier alone consumed two six-packs and was drunk. Due to other events, which took place same day they had an argument when they returned home from their night out. Defendant stated that he tried to leave to avoid further quarrel but Mrs. Bier stood in the bedroom doorway, to block him from leaving. Defendant went in the closet, pulled a gun from its holster, cocked it and placed it on the bed and said that to stop him she'd have to shoot him. When defendant turned away, Mrs. Bier picked the gun and pointed it at her head with her finger on the trigger. Defendant shouted, "That damn thing's loaded." To prevent its aim, defendant tried to grab or slap the gun from Mrs. Bier but it discharged and Mrs. Bier collapsed on the floor.

Defendant was charged with negligent homicide and he pleaded not guilty. His defense was that based on the angle of the bullet's path, it is impossible that he held the gun when it went off. He also claimed the state failed to prove the required mental state and causation elements for negligent homicide.

The court affirmed the conviction on the ground that, negligent homicide only requires a gross deviation from a reasonable standard of care, that defendant's conduct in pulling out, cocking and throwing a loaded gun within reach of his intoxicated wife, was grossly negligent. The risk created by the defendant's conduct under the circumstances, was a foreseeable risk, deserving criminal liability.

Note: Find the entire case using the case number above for the complete case history and court opinion.

QUESTIONS

[1] Consider the different approaches to unintended homicide discussed earlier and apply the four differing views to the defendant Bier. What is the correlation between the approaches and the conviction of negligent homicide? Your answer must be convincing and legibly stated in the space provided. Discuss the best approach you would prefer in an unintended negligent homicide case, for example, in the state of New York.

Notes:

[2] Janet is fascinated by her husband Jason's position as a police sergeant. In fact, she likes to play police sometimes in his uniform. Jason has just arrived from one of his shifts and after removing his uniform with the gun still in the holster; he came to the table for dinner. Janet wanted to surprise him as usual so she changed into his uniform, took the gun from its holster and as she entered the living room pointing the gun at him jokingly, she said to Jason: "Stop eating you are under arrest darling." Her finger accidentally pressed the trigger when she heard a loud siren of a police car just passing by in the street; there was a bang and a bullet hit Jason in the head killing him instantly. Janet had cooked dinner for Jason so she had oil residues on her fingers, giving her fingers more freedom of movement than usual. Based on the facts, is Janet guilty of murder in the death of Jason? If yes explain and if not, what is the possible crime Janet can be charged with? Discuss your answer below.

Notes:

[3] Considering the facts in the Jason's case, assume Janet is charged with negligent homicide, what is the relationship between the risk factor in her action and the crime she is charged with?

[4] *Bimbola* was driving home from a friend's house when suddenly she lost control of her SUV. The vehicle rolled over the sidewalk killing Kate who was six months pregnant. The baby was quickly delivered by emergency C-section but died afterwards. Tests later showed *Bimbola* had a heavy dose of cocaine in her system at the time of the accident. Is *Bimbola* guilty of murder or negligent homicide? How culpable is she for the death of the baby?

NOTE: For the statutory offense of "automobile homicide" that is causing a fatal traffic accident while under the influence of liquor or drug, see *State v. Twitchell, 8 Utah 2d 314, 333 P.2d 1075 (1959)*. Also, vehicular homicide as a result of drunken driven is a violation of Motor Vehicle homicide statute and not the general manslaughter statute. *Lopez v. State, 586 P.2d 157 (Wyo.1978)*; however, this may be subject to change depending on state law.

STATE V. SETY

Court of Appeals of Arizona, Division I, Department A, 1979
121 Ariz. 354, 590 P.2d 470

In the morning hours of March 19, 1976, Donald Cue died as the result of injuries inflicted by the appellant, David Sety, during a bizarre series of confrontations at an isolated campground. Appellant was tried on an open charge of murder. During trial the court granted a directed verdict of acquittal as to first-degree murder, and the jury convicted the appellant of second-degree murder. On post trial motions, the trial court reduced the charge to voluntary manslaughter and sentenced Sety to serve not less than nine nor more than ten years in the Arizona State Prison.

Appellant Sety appeals from the judgment and sentence, and the State appeals from the trial court's reduction of the conviction from second-degree murder to voluntary manslaughter. We affirm the conviction and modify the sentence.

On the day in question, the appellant was camping alone in an area below Bartlett Lake Dam in Maricopa County, Arizona. At approximately 6:00 a.m., the intoxicated victim, Mr. Cue, awakened him and engaged him in a rambling discussion, primarily about weapons. Cue admired the appellant's hunting knife, asked Sety to sharpen Cue's own knife and boasted of having killed eight people with that knife. Sety said that he was shaking by this talk and that he crawled into his camper to get a pistol. Sety stated that as he emerged from the camper Cue was pointing a gun directly at his head and laughing in a threatening manner...

After other threatening attempts by Cue on Sety, the appellant fired, striking Cue in the side, told Cue he was making a citizen's arrest and ordered him to begin walking toward the dam keeper's house. The two men then left the site near the camper, referred to at the trial as site A, and proceeded toward the house. The physical evidence and Sety's testimony up to that point are not in dispute. The State does not contend that Sety was guilty of any culpable conduct prior to the time that the men left site A...

After series of other events, Sety stated that he choked the victim into unconsciousness, went back to the camper to reload his pistol and then returned to where Cue was lying, designated during trial as site B...Sety claimed that his gun discharged striking Cue in the head. Certain at last that Cue was dead Sety continued to the dam keeper's house and reported the homicide to the Sheriff's Department.

Sety claimed that the wounds, which he inflicted upon Cue after they left site B were all either in self-defense or in justified furtherance of a citizen's arrest. He argued that, based upon his testimony, he should have been acquitted of all charges.

The physical evidence, however, does not fully support Sety's version of what transpired after Cue and Sety left site B. This evidence contradicted Sety's proffered defenses, making the court to conclude that the evidence presented was sufficient to find criminal culpability.

The court agreed that the provocation and terror, which caused the killing, were instigated by the intrusion of Cue into the pre-dawn solitude of the appellant's campground, making the case a classic illustration of manslaughter resulting from mitigating circumstances.

However, on the issue of whether the amount of force used by Sety was excessive under the circumstances, the court stated its belief that there was sufficient evidence for the jury to reject Sety's defenses and to convict him of manslaughter, but that the evidence did not support a murder conviction. At most, appellant was guilty of excessive retaliation constituting manslaughter rather than murder.

In conclusion, the court affirmed the conviction and ruled that the trial court's reduction of the conviction from second-degree murder to voluntary manslaughter, was mandated by the evidence.

Note: Please find the case using the case number provided to read the entire case and full opinion of the court.

NOTES AND QUESTIONS

[1] Chris and David found they were both dating the same girl a local Miss. Brooklyn. Both decided the other should not have her and as a result a quarrel ensued. They agreed to settle their differences in a park not far from Chris's house. During the fight, David overpowered Chris with an uppercut, which left Chris bleeding and embarrassed. Chris went into his house, got a hammer and struck David twice in the head knocking him completely unconscious. He decided that was not enough and hit him three more times until David could no longer move. David was rushed to the emergency where he died on arrival. Is Chris guilty of murder or manslaughter? To answer consider the notes below.

[2] The proof of the intention to kill, and of the disposition of mind constituting murder in the first degree, under the Act of Assembly, lies on the Commonwealth. But this proof need not be express or positive. It may be inferred from the circumstances. If, from all the facts attending the killing, the jury can fully, reasonably, and satisfactorily infer the existence of the intention to kill, and the malice of heart with which it was done, they will be warranted in so doing. He who uses upon the body of another, at some vital part, with a manifest intention to use it upon him, a deadly weapon, as an axe, a gun, a knife or a pistol, must in the absence of qualifying facts, be presumed to know that his blow is likely to kill; and knowing this, must be presumed to intend the death, which is the probable and ordinary consequence of such an act. He, who so uses a deadly weapon without a sufficient cause of provocation, must be presumed to do it wickedly, or from a bad heart. Therefore, he who takes the life of another with a deadly weapon, and with a manifest design thus to use it upon him, with sufficient time to deliberate, and fully to form the conscious purpose of killing, and without any sufficient reason or cause of extenuation, is guilty of murder in the first degree.[38]

[3] All murder not of the first degree, is necessarily of the second degree, and includes all unlawful killing under circumstances of depravity of heart, and a disposition of mind regardless of social duty; but where no intention to kill exists or can be reasonably and fully inferred. Therefore, in all cases of murder, if no intention to kill can be inferred or collected from the circumstances, the verdict must be murder in the second degree.[39]

---

[38] *Commonwealth v. Drum*, Supreme Court of Pennsylvania 58 Pa. 9 (1868)
[39] *Commonwealth v. Drum*, supra

[4] Manslaughter is the unlawful killing of another without malice express or implied. Manslaughter may be voluntary in a sudden heat, or involuntary, but in the commission of an unlawful act.

[5] Consider question (1) above carefully, how applicable is notes (2), (3) and (4) above to the facts of the case? Determine which best describe the crime Chris could be charged with. Explain your answers in an essay below but before, choose the right answer from the following question.

Based on facts of the case, Chris is guilty of what crime?

(A) **Murder for using a deadly weapon to avenge David's uppercut**

(B) **Murder for using a deadly weapon multiple times on David, while he had time to deliberate**

(C) **Second degree murder because he did not intend to kill David**

(D) **Manslaughter because Chris acted in the heat of passion in response to David's uppercut**

(E) **None of the above.**

Notes:

Notes:

Notes: Read the following question and choose the correct answer from the list that follows.

Wolf was married to Becky for 32 years. Becky had Cancer she was hospitalized and later placed on life support. After several sessions of chemotherapy, her condition remained terminal, the Cancer had metastasized and she was having a lot of pain. All medications prescribed failed to stop the pain so, she begged Wolf to do something to help relieve her pain. Wolf pleaded with Becky's physician to remove her life support but the hospital refused to comply. One early morning while Becky was in bed sleeping, Wolf came in unannounced and remove the life support. Due to Wolf's action, Becky was unable to breath and died shortly after.

What crime is Wolf guilty of at Common law?

   (A) Wolf is not guilty of Becky's death because Cancer killed Becky

   (B) Wolf is guilty of Manslaughter because he had no intent to kill Becky

   (C) Not guilty because he was only helping to relieve Becky's pain

   (D) Not guilty because Wolf acted out of compassion for his wife

   (E) Wolf is guilty of murder because he acted with intent and caused Becky's death.

Notes: The following is a case involving a mistaken identity, which led to a homicide. Go through the question and select your choice from the alternatives.

George was so mad at Kenneth for stealing his watch the other day. He came up behind Tyson who looked exactly like Kenneth and struck him on the head with the palm of his hand. Unbeknownst, he had hit Tyson a professional knife thrower not Kenneth. George realized he was wrong and apologized but Tyson was too angry to accept his apology. He lunged at George with a knife that killed George instantly.

Tyson is guilty of what crime if any?

    (A) No crime because George attacked him first

    (B) No crime because George intended to kill Kenneth when he struck the wrong guy

    (C) Tyson guilty of murder for using excessive force and a deadly weapon to respond to a slap to the head

    (D) Tyson guilty of murder for use of asymmetrical force

    (E) C and D above

    (F) None of the above

Chapter Six
Homicide By Unlawful Act

The Felony Murder Rule

At common law, one who is responsible for unintended death of another, during the perpetration or attempted commission of a felony was guilty of murder. This became the *Felony Murder-Rule*. At the time, most felonies were punishable by death since such crimes were considered dangerous to human life. The threat posed by such felonies warranted strict response and as a result, the threats serve as a justification for the harshness of the rule. Under the Felony murder rule, a death, which occurs by accident (unintended) or chance during the course of the commission of a *felony*, is first-degree murder. However, this is a common law doctrine the rule has since been modified by statutes in some jurisdictions. The reasons for the modifications was due to the fact that the common law rule, became too harsh as it applied to all felonies irrespective of the dangerousness and threat to human life. Nowadays, courts only apply the rule to specific felonies considered to be of the largest threat to human life; among such categories of crime are rape, arson, kidnapping, robbery, and mayhem.

Take for example the following scenario, George and Ben decide to rob a TARGET store, both think it would be necessary to use all force at their disposer to carry out the robbery. During the commission of the crime, a security officer attempted to stop them but was shot by George accidentally and died at the scene. Under the felony murder rule, both George and Ben are guilty of murder even though, Ben did not fire the fatal shot. They are equally culpable for the murder irrespective of whether or not Ben conspired with George to kill the security office.

In the case above, the rule acts to provide the specific intent required for the defendants to be culpable for the murder, it creates a form of vicarious liability between both felons. Even though, death in this case was not intended, the defendants may be found culpable based on the principle that, one who engages in inherently dangerous crimes should be aware of the high risk created by such crime to human life; such that, all those involved are equally liable for the resulting homicide.

To establish a felony murder in most jurisdiction today, it must be shown that: (1) the defendant was engaged in the commission or attempted commission of a specified felony; (2) a death must have occurred during the commission or attempted commission of the felony and: (3) the death must be as a result of the felony meaning that, but for the crime, the death would not have occurred.

There are different views on the application of the felony murder rule. One view posits that, the rule is intended to deter negligent and accidental killings during perpetration of felonies. The argument is that co-felons will dissuade each other from the use of violence knowing they could be liable for murder.

The other postulate is directed not towards the killing but on the felony itself; it endorses the rule as a deterrent to dangerous felonies. The notion is that by punishing both accidental and deliberate killings resulting from a felony is 'the strongest possible deterrent' to curbing inherently dangerous felonies.[40]

'The felony murder rule is a theory of transferred or constructive intent. Under this theory, the intent to commit the felony is transferred to the act of killing in order to find culpability for the homicide'[41]. The rule serves the objective of relieving the State of the burden of proving premeditation or malice, which is required in most first-degree murder cases for a conviction to stand.

In most States, the lawmakers specified by statutes what crime must be committed for the felony murder rule to take effect. Some however, have limited the rule to those felonies recognized at common law.

In some instances, it may be essential to certify when a crime began and when it ended for the felony murder rule to apply. Take for example the following scenario: George has just entered a home and robbed a woman of her purse and belongings. He was running away chased by a Police Officer on foot; As the Police Officer tried to avoid an incoming traffic, he was struck and killed by a motorist. The question is whether the death occurred during the commission of the crime, such that, George may be guilty of murder. In most cases the answer is yes; the officer died during the commission of a felony in this case, robbery. Moreover, there is a causal connection between

---

[40] Nelson E. Roth & Scott E. Sundby, *The Felony Murder Rule: A Doctrine of Constitutional Crossroads*, 70 *Cornell L. Rev. 446, 450-58* (1985)
[41] Wayne R. LaFave, *Modern Criminal Law* supra: P. 323, note 1.

the crime and the death since but for the crime, the death would not have occurred. Proving that the crime occurred during the commission or attempted commission of a felony will satisfy requirement (2) above.

In the same Scenario, suppose that the Police Officer was driving fast to respond to the robbery, he ran the red light and struck an incoming vehicle killing a 78 years old woman. Is this during the commission of the crime? It is unlikely that a felony murder would be found, since the death was too far removed from the commission or attempted commission of the felony. George may not be feloniously culpable for the death.

Also to satisfy requirement (3), the felony must be the legal or *proximate* cause of the death. The causal connection must be closely linked and the death must be a "consequence not coincidence" of the criminal act. Not only that, the death must also be a foreseeable consequence of the felonious act. Suppose Dele broke into a house at 2:00 A.M. with the intention to rob the inhabitants and the 86 years old woman inside suffered a shock from fear and died when she suddenly saw Dele breaking into the home. Dele is guilty of felony murder because his felonious act precipitated the resulting death. However, if Benson a neighbor of the woman unaware of the robbery suffered a shock and dies, Dele is not guilty of felony murder. The simultaneous occurrence does not establish a causal connection between the death and his felonious act. He is therefore, not culpable for the neighbor's death under the felony murder rule.

In some jurisdictions, the event that precipitated the death of the victim need not occur as a result of the action of one of the perpetrators of the crime. If Biola and Stephen decide to rob a Home Depot and as a result are engage in a shootout with the police and the police accidentally shot an innocent shopper to death. Biola and Stephen are equally guilty of murder of the innocent shopper under the felony-murder rule. The officer is not guilty of any crime because both Biola and Stephen set in motion the series of events, which led to the death of the innocent shopper. In other situations, it may happen that the police accidentally kill one of the felons for example, if the police during a shootout accidentally killed Biola; Stephen is not guilty of the felony-murder of Biola. However, he may be charged with robbery.

The felony murder-rule recognize vicarious liability of co-felons however, there is limitation. If a defendant can establish by clear and convincing evidence that he did not engage in the act, which caused the death; did not conspire to cause the death, plan, or encourage the act of his co-felon; and had no reason to believe the act would be committed, he may have a defense to felony-murder charge in some states. The reason for such rule is that, there are situations where a co-conspirator decides at the last minute to withdraw from the act without doing more; but as a co-conspirator he is still considered part of the act if he did not take further action for example, to report the situation to the police or appropriate authority. The rules concerning accomplices, parties and principals to crimes may establish culpability irrespective of the felony-murder rule.

In jurisdictions that subscribed to the felony-murder rule, all killings that occur during or attempted commission of a named felony are categorized as first-degree murder. All other killings that occur during other felonies are considered second-degree murder. A named felony can be in the following category: rape, arson, aggravated robbery, mayhem, and kidnapping specifically, those felonies creating the largest threat to human life.

CONRAD V. STATE

Supreme Court of Ohio, 1906
75 Ohio St. 52, 78 N.E. 957

It was charged in the indictment that the plaintiff broke into a dwelling house at night with intent to take and carry away personal property, which was in the dwelling; and that while in the perpetration of such burglary, the plaintiff shot and killed one Daniel E. Davis.

The argument in this case is that the perpetration of the burglary was complete when the house was entered, or at least while the burglars were within the house, and that as they carried nothing away in their flight the crime of burglary was complete when they left the house. The body of Officer Davis was found twenty-five or thirty feet from the house and on another lot. Therefore, it is argued, the killing was not in the perpetration of a burglary and therefore, not felony murder.

The court rejected the argument based on the principle that, when a person takes with force and violence the goods of another from his person or presence and against his will, he has committed robbery. … but it does not necessarily complete the crime. It constitutes robbery so far as to render the perpetrator liable to conviction for it. However, the *act of robbery itself may be prolonged beyond the time when that liability is fixed.*

Citing other cases involving killing before, during and after the technical perfection of the collateral crime, the opinion indicated that courts practically concur in the view expressed by the Court of Appeals of New York that, if a defendant while engaged in securing his plunder, or in *any of the acts immediately connected with his crime, he kills anyone resisting him, the defendant is guilty of murder under the statute* (Dolan v. People,).

In conclusion, the court affirmed the circuit court's decision citing the opinion that when the homicide is committed within the *res gestae* [42] of the felony charged, it is committed in the perpetration of, or attempt to perpetrate, the felony, within the meaning of the statute" (Bissot v. State,).

---

[42] "The res gestae embraces not only the actual facts of the transaction and the circumstances surrounding it, but the matters immediately antecedent to and having a direct causal connection with it, as well as acts immediately following it and so closely connected with it as to form in reality a part of the occurrence." *State v. Fouquette, 67 Nev. 505, 221 P.2d 404, 417 (1950)*

Note: Research the case to read the whole case history and opinion of the court.

NOTES & QUESTIONS

[1] John, Dave, and Dare decide to rob the Take Two Strip Club in Miami owned by Chris. After a recent robbery in the club, Chris got a license and was allowed to carry a gun for his protection and the security of his club. The defendants are aware of Chris' routine so they came at 5:30AM to hide behind a dumpster located at the back of the club, waiting for Chris to arrive at 6:00AM when he normally counts the money from previous night. As Chris entered the club, the defendants overpowered him and in the process a shot was fired killing Chris instantly. John later confessed that he fired the fatal shot. A search of his house revealed a shotgun that turned out not to be the murder weapon in fact, investigation revealed the victim's own gun was used to kill him and that Bimpe a receptionist at the club was the mastermind. John is now claiming that he acted in self-defense and that since the victim's own gun was used to commit the crime, he should only be charged with robbery. Does John have a good defense? What crime can John be charged with? Are Dave and Dare guilty of any crime? Remember neither of them fired the fatal shot. Should they just be charged with robbery since they only accompany John and have no hand in the actual killing? Is Bimpe the mastermind guilty of any crime? Write a one-page essay below describing your response to all the questions.

Based on the facts of this case, what crime can Bimpe be charged with from the list below? Remember that to withdraw from a crime initially orchestrated by a defendant, the defendant must not only announce her intent to withdraw to her co-conspirators, in some cases, she is required to go a step further such as, informing the authority about a potential crime.

Based on this principle, Bimpe is guilty of:

(A) **Felony murder and can be equally charged with the others**
(B) **Felony murder and conspiracy to commit a felony**
(C) **Not guilty of any crime because she did not participate in both crime and murder**
(D) **Guilty only of conspiracy to commit a felony since John lacked the intent to kill**
(E) **Guilty of manslaughter and conspiracy**
(F) **None of the above.**

Notes:

[2] Same scenario above however, all evidence show that though, she masterminded the entire robbery, Bimpe later withdrew from the entire plan in fact, she had no idea or believe that John, Dave, and Dare would follow through with the plan to rob the Take Two club. Based on such evidence, should Bimpe go free without any charge? Explain your answers to question 1 and 2 below with concrete reference to the felony-murder rule.

Notes:

[3] So far, one state has abandoned the felony-murder rule leaving the jury to decide based on evidence whether the rule should apply in felony cases resulting in death. However, juries may have to show that *malice* exists for the rule to apply. In *People v. Aaron, 409 Mich. 672, 299 N.W.2d 304 (1980)*, the court stated that it is no longer acceptable to equate the intent to commit a felony with the intent to kill, intent to do great bodily harm, or wanton and willful disregard of the likelihood that the natural tendency of a person's behavior is to cause death or great bodily harm. In *People v. Hansen, 368 Mich. 344, 350, 118 N.W.2d (1962)*, the court said that malice, requires an intent to cause the very harm that results or some harm of the same general nature, or an act done in wanton or willful disregard of the plaintiff and strong likelihood that such harm will result. In a charge of felony murder, it is the murder, which is the harm, which is being punished. A defendant who only intends to commit the felony does not intend to commit the harm that results and may or may not be guilty of perpetrating an act done in wanton or willful disregard of the plain and strong likelihood that such harm will result. Although the circumstances surrounding the commission of the felony may evidence a greater intent beyond the intent to commit the felony, or a wanton and willful act in disregard of the possible consequence of death or serious injury, the intent to commit the felony, of itself does not connote a 'man-endangering-state-of-mind.' Hence, it does not suffice that the intent to commit a felony, constitutes a sufficient *mens rea* to establish the crime of murder.

In its ruling, the court held that malice is the intention to kill, the intention to do great bodily harm, or wanton and willful disregard of the likelihood that the natural tendency of defendant's behavior is to cause death or great bodily harm. It further held that malice is an essential element of any murder, as that term is judicially defined, whether the murder occurs in the course of a felony or otherwise. The facts and circumstances involved in the perpetration of a felony may evidence an intent to kill, an intent to cause great bodily harm, or a wanton or willful disregard of the likelihood that the natural tendency of defendant's behavior is to cause death or great bodily harm. However, the decision must be left to the jury to infer from all the evidence. Otherwise, a jury might be required to find the fact of malice, when they were satisfied from the whole evidence that malice is lacking.

Notes:

[4] Based on the court's opinion in *Hansen* and *Aaron* above, think about the following scenario. Curtis and Peter planned to rob the BJ store downtown Brooklyn. Both decided they would use every means possible to be successful and avoid capture. In fact, Curtis said, "If the armed security guard or anybody comes in the way, they will have it." Both armed with a knife and a 48 Caliber approached the store. While casing the store, they met Janet entering the store with her 15 months old baby. Curtis pretending to be a customer, said hi to Janet and the baby at the entrance. 15 minutes after, they entered the store ordering everyone to freeze the security officer saw the event from a distance and attempts to draw his gun but was quickly shot in the arm by Curtis. The bullet passed through and hit Janet's 15 months old baby who died instantly. Assume both Curtis and Peter live in a state that has abandoned the felony-murder rule but subscribed to the court's opinion above in order to find the rule applicable; are Curtis and Peter guilty of felony-murder or attempted murder or both? Is the evidence sufficient enough for the jury to establish malice necessary to find both guilty of murder of the baby under the felony-murder rule and attempted murder of the security officer? Explain in the space below with proper reference to the court's opinion in *Aaron* and *Hansen*.

Notes:

[5] Based on the evidence above, should Curtis and Peter also be charged with robbery? Or do you think the robbery charge should *merge* so that both are only charged with murder?

In *State v. Thompson, 88 Wash.2d 13, 558 P.2d 202* (1977), the defendant was found guilty of felony-murder of her husband based on the theory that the death occurred as a result of her felonious assault upon her husband. On appeal, the court indicated that states, which have considered the question have adopted the merger rule, resulting in a holding that only felonies independent of the homicide can support a felony murder conviction. The court however, refused to reject earlier Washington decision to the contrary.

Notes: Read the following question and select the right answer among the choices.

Paul, Betty and Brian entered a Giant store at midnight drawing their weapons and demanding that the cashier place all money in the register in a bag they provided. Patton a store employee saw the robbery in motion and triggered the alarm that brought the local police to the scene. In an attempt to escape Betty shot and killed Douglas, a responding officer. Paul, Betty and Brian have all been charged with felony murder. Paul and Brian claim they should only be charged with the robbery since it was Betty who shot and killed Douglas.

    (A) Paul and Brian not guilty of felony murder
    (B) Paul and Brian guilty of robbery not felony murder
    (C) Paul and Brian equally guilty of felony murder
    (D) Only Betty is guilty since she fired the fatal shot
    (E) Only (B) and (C) are correct

Assume that Betty is charged with the felony murder of Douglas, under which of the following situations is Betty most likely to be convicted.

    (A) Douglas is shot and killed by Paul
    (B) Douglas is shot and killed by Brian
    (C) Brian is intentionally shot and killed by Betty
    (D) Brian is shot and killed by officer Douglas
    (E) Only (A) and (B)

[6] Carol a Miss Brooklyn, New York has been engaged to her boyfriend Scott for more than a year. To seal their love, Scott gave Carol an engagement ring and both planned to get married, in a year or two. Unbeknownst, Scott was also engaged to Rebecca whom Carol considered a friend of Scott'. When Carol learnt that Scott had given a ring to Rebecca and confronted him about it, he denied the allegations. Carol did not believe him so she decided to visit Rebecca to tell her to lay off her boyfriend. As Carol jumped in her car, Scott followed in a different car to stop her from causing him embarrassment in front of Rebecca. On arrival at Rebecca's house Carol approached Rebecca gently and told her to stop dating Scott. Few minutes to the conversation, Scott arrived at Rebecca's doorstep and an argument ensued between Scott and Carol. Carol infuriated at Scott's comments reached in her car and pulled out a pistol warning Scott she would shoot him. Scott then retreated to his car and few seconds later a shot was heard. As Rebecca opened the door to enter her apartment, Scott approached her bleeding profusely from the upper part of his leg and yelled at Rebecca to call 911 to be taken to the hospital. On arrival at the emergency, doctors found that one of Scott's arteries has been badly damaged and Scott was losing a lot of blood. They tried to insert a tube in his chest to help control the bleeding but in the process another artery was severed causing more bleeding and his death three days later. Carol indicated she shot Scott because she thought he was reaching for a gun in his car however, a search of Scott's car reveal none. Evidence also shows Scott was indeed engaged to Rebecca at the same time to Carol. Based on these facts, Carol is guilty of what crime? Assume Carol is charged with felony-murder of Scott, can she be guilty? How is a *felony* murder charge possible in this case? What is or are basis for the *felony* in this case? Assume that Carol is found not guilty, what best arguments supports her case? Is Rebecca guilty of any crime? This is a two-page essay. Describe your thoughts in the space below.

Notes:

STATE V. LOSEY

23 Ohio App. 3d 93, 491 N.E.2d 379 (1985)

According to the defendant, he came to a house located at 616 Whitehorne Avenue shortly after 11:00 PM on November 25, 1983. He knocked at the front door and when he got no response, he forced open the door and attempted to remove a bicycle. His friend, who was waiting outside, called that a car was slowly approaching the house. The defendant then placed the bicycle beside the front door and left, leaving the front door open behind him. James Harper, the owner of 616 Whitehorne Avenue, stated that he heard a noise at approximately 1:00 AM and thereafter, his mother with whom he lived, appeared at his bedroom door inquiring about the noise. They both went into the living room, where they discovered the open front door and the bicycle standing near the door. James Harper stated that he told his mother to go back to her bedroom while he went to check the rest of the house. After checking, he came back to the living room and was calling the police when his mother appeared in the hallway looking very upset and then collapsed. Mrs. Harper later died after efforts to revive her failed. Prior to the burglary, Mrs. Harper had returned from bingo at approximately 10:00 PM that evening and had gone to bed.

Based on these facts, defendant was found guilty of aggravated burglary and involuntary manslaughter. Defendant appealed the Trial court's decision claiming that: the court's decision does not support the evidence, that his action was not the proximate cause of death and that the court erred in finding him guilty of involuntary manslaughter.

Defendant argued that the judgment should be reversed, because Mrs. Harper's death was not the proximate result of his conduct.

The court rejected defendant's arguments, finding a causal connection. According to the court, defendant's conduct was a cause of Mrs. Harper's death in the sense that it set in motion events, which culminated in her death. In its opinion, the events that led to Mrs. Harper's death was within the scope of the risk created by defendant's conduct, as illustrated by the facts of *State v. Chambers, 53 Ohio App. 2d 266* (1977)[43]

---

[43] In *State v. Chambers, supra* the defendant and a confederate broke into a resident, were confronted by the armed resident and, in the melee which ensued, defendant's confederate was mortally wounded by the resident. Determining that the companion's death was a foreseeable consequence of defendant's conduct, the Court of Appeals upheld his conviction for involuntary manslaughter.

In its final ruling, the court overruled defendant's assignments of error and affirmed judgment of the trial court.

Note: Student should research the case for the entire case history and court's opinion.

QUESTIONS

[1] Assume that in the *Losey* case Mrs. Harper did not detect the events that ensued at all but was informed 40 minutes later by her son after defendant had left the scene. Will the defendant still be guilty as charged? Explain your answer with reference to *duration* of the felony in the space provided but first choose the right answer from the followings.

IF Mrs. Harper learnt about the events 40 minutes after and then suffered a shock and died, will defendant still be responsible for her death?

- **(A) Yes, defendant is responsible no matter what**
- **(B) No, defendant's conduct would be too improbable and remote to form the basis for criminal sanction**
- **(C) Yes, because defendant's action is the proximate cause of death**
- **(D) Yes, defendant's action set in motion the circumstances that caused death**
- **(E) None of the above**

Notes:

[2] Read *People v. Gladman, 41 N.Y.2d 123, 390* (1976). How is that case applicable to *Losey* if at all? Explain.

Notes:

[3] Rashida and her husband Tunde like to play what they call the *Kinky Game* before intimacy. During the game, one is tied to a chair in handcuffs and blindfolded while the other touches with any object that the one blindfolded must recognize. The first to be handcuffed and blindfolded was Rashida. Tunde touched her with the TV remote, which she quickly recognized, winning her first round. However, on Tunde's turn, Rashida plunged a knife in his chest, Tunde felt a great pain but could not move being in handcuffs and blindfolded. Tunde asked to be untied immediately as blood starts to come down his chest but Rashida said she lost the keys to the handcuffs. He asked her to call 911 but she said the 911 operators did not pick the phone. Finally, she located the keys and as she drove to a hospital nearby, she stopped the car on the way and plunged the knife in his chest once more. Passersby later rescued Tunde but he died on arrival to the hospital. Rashida is now claiming her husband's death was a mistake that it was a result of a "stupid game." Evidence show that Rashida had been dating a co-worker, prior to her husband's death and that her plan, was to get rid of her husband for the other man.

Based on these facts, is Rashida guilty of murder? If not what possible crime can she be charged with? Is there any evidence of malice or intent to kill in this case? Explain your answers with proper analysis.

Notes: Based on the facts provided and the circumstances of the case, write your answer below.

[4] Jennifer and George have been married for ten years. Both have three children and seem to love their children very much. However, the ten years of marriage has brought nothing to Jennifer but abuse by George in fact, neighbors are very much privy to the abuse and on several occasions, Jennifer called the police to their home and got George arrested three times in which George, was jailed for couple of days each time. On the last abuse, the police was called to the home, they found Jennifer bound and tied to a pole in the basement. She told the police she had been there for 3 days under constant abuse by George. Ironically, Jennifer was always the one to let George out of jail because she feared he might do something to her if not released soon and also because of their children. A year has passed and no one saw any trace of George in the neighborhood. Jennifer was questioned about where her husband went, she indicated he had left her for another woman and got involved with drugs. Unsatisfied, neighbors called the police to verify. On entering the home, they found the decomposed body of George in a locked room lying in bed face down as if in a sleep, with a bullet wound to the back of the head. Jennifer claimed she acted in self-defense to prevent further abuse, but evidence from the scene revealed George was face down in a sleep mode when he was shot in the back of the head. Based on these facts, what crime can Jennifer be charged with? How likely is a charge of manslaughter in this case? Is there any mitigating factor to reduce her charge? Assume Jennifer, is charged with murder is this a proper charge? If so explain and if not state why. Your answers must include any defense you think Jennifer might have.

[5] Kate and Nicolas have been married for 5 years. Kate brought two teenage daughters into the marriage adopted by her husband. The couples also have two sons together. Both Kate and Nicolas are *swingers*, they belonged to a group where each couple meet routinely and exchange their partners for sexual pleasures. On many of the routine encounters, Kate was involved with another member of the group Stephen, the sexual encounters later developed into a relationship, which Nicolas did not like. He talked over it with Kate however, the relationship became serious and Kate did not let go. She indicated to one of her teenage daughters Catherine a 15- year- old that she has fallen in love with Stephen and would like to get rid of her husband. A week after, Nicolas was found dead in his sleep with two gunshot wounds to the head and chest. Evidence revealed that Kate purchased a pistol and encouraged Catherine to do the killing on her behalf. She told her that being 15-year- old, she would only be charged as a minor or even let go. For her cooperation with investigation, Catherine received a 36 years reduced sentence. Kate is now

claiming no involvement in the killing that it was all planned and carried out by Catherine. All evidence, point to the fact that Catherine indeed fired the two shots. Based on the facts, is Kate guilty of murder? Explain your answer with analysis. Is there any chance of mitigation? What other crime can Kate be charged with? Explain why.

Notes:

Chapter Seven

The Theory Of Causation

From the tort theory of negligence we learn that besides proving duty and breach of duty, the prosecution must also establish proximate cause. It must show that the defendant's action or omission is the legal cause of injury suffered by the victim. Likewise, in criminal law, there must be a causal connection between the act and the harmful result. In any civilized criminal justice, liability cannot be enforced on a defendant unless it is determined the action punished, is in some degree a result of his act. Imagine one charged with murder and sentenced to life imprisonment when all evidence shows that his action did not cause the victim's death. In fact, it is fair to say that such a sentence is far from proper justice. The issue is not what people say is the cause but rather what the law says is the cause of the victim's demise.

"It has been said that an act, which in no way contributed to the result in question cannot be a cause of it; but this of course, does not mean that an event, which *might* have happened in the same way though the defendant's act or omission had not occurred, is not a result of it. The question is not what would have happened, but what did happen."[44]

What is essential here is that, whenever a crime requires the occurrence of specific conduct for its commission to be established, it is important that defendant's conduct be the "legal or proximate" cause of the result or else no culpability can be found. For example, the crime of homicide requires the death of a human being therefore, defendant's action must be the cause of death to establish culpability. This is to say that but for defendant's action or omission, the result (death) would not have occurred.

"A primary requisite to either criminal or civil liability is that the act of the defendant be the cause in fact of the injury. This requirement is embodied in the familiar *causa sine qua non* rule, generally called the 'but for' rule. This test generally is satisfactory when applied in negative form, and it is a basic principle that a defendant is not liable unless the injury would not have resulted but for his wrongful act. But as an affirmative test the 'but for' rule provides no infallible standard and does not constitute a fair test of liability in the absence of further qualification. ...

---

[44] Beale, *The Proximate Consequences of An Act*, 33 Harv.Law Rev 633, 638 (1920)

"The modern authorities, while agreed that the 'but for' test is inadequate differ materially in their concepts of proximate causation. The theories conveniently may be placed in two groups. One group seeks the necessary connection between the result and the act; the other, between the result and the actor's mind."[45]

To establish proximate cause three tests are required: *Intention, probability*, and the *absence of an independent-intervening force*. "Any intended consequence of an act is proximate. It would plainly be absurd that a person should be allowed to act with an intention to produce a certain consequence, and then when that very consequence in fact follows his act, to escape liability for it on the plea that it was not proximate.

"Probability … is a name for someone's opinion or guess as to whether a consequence will result. …

"The person whose opinion is taken is a reasonable and prudent man in the situation of the actor. …

"The third test of proximateness is the non-intervention of an independent cause between the original cause and the consequence in question. … Therefore it will be convenient to call it an isolating cause."[46]

To establish his negligent act did not cause death, a defendant must show something else happened in the form of an independent force that caused the death. Here, the defendant must establish an independent superior force, cuts through the chain of causation and therefore, became the cause of death to avoid liability.

Normally, in negligent cases, prove of a separate intervening force as the cause of death may exculpate the defendant or make him partially liable. Even in such cases, the foreign force must be equal to the defendant's action to share liability. However, if the intervening force is a dominant force the defendant may not be culpable. Nonetheless, the defendant must still show that he did not set in motion the events that led to victim's death.

[45] Focht, *Proximate Cause In the Law of Homicide-With Special Reference to California Cases, 12 So.Cal.L.Rev. 19,* 20-21 (1938)
[46] Terry, *Proximate Consequences in the Law of Torts, 28 Harv.L.Rev. 10, 17-20 (1914)* quoted from Rollin M. Perkins et al. Criminal Law and Procedure, 6th edition (1984) P. 410

PEOPLE V. LEWIS

Supreme Court of California, Department Two, 1899
124 Cal. 551, 57 P. 470

The defendant was convicted of manslaughter and appeals from the judgment and from an order refusing a new trial. Based on facts, defendant and deceased were brother-in-law, and not friendly, although they were on speaking and visiting terms. On the morning of the homicide the deceased visited the resident of the defendant, was received in a friendly manner, but after a while an altercation arose, as a result, defendant shot deceased in the abdomen, inflicting a wound that was necessarily mortal. Farrell fell to the ground, stunned for an instant, but soon got up and went into the house, saying: "shoot me again; I shall die anyway." His strength soon failed him and he was put to bed. Soon afterwards, when no other person was present except a lad about nine years of age, nephew of the deceased and son of the defendant, the deceased procured a knife and cut his own throat, inflicting a ghastly wound, from the effect of which according to the medical evidence, he must necessarily have died in five minutes. The wound inflicted by the defendant severed the mesenteric artery, and medical witnesses testified that under the circumstances it was necessarily mortal, and death would ensue within one hour from the effects of the wound alone. Medical witnesses thought that the knife wound accelerated death.

The argument put forward by the defense was that this is a case where one languishing from a mortal wound is killed by an intervening cause, and, therefore, Lewis did not kill deceased. The attorney general does not controvert the general proposition contended for, but argued that the wound inflicted by the defendant was the direct cause of the throat cutting, and, therefore, defendant is criminally liable for the death.

The Supreme Court affirmed the lower court's decision, finding no error in the judgment. Based on its opinion, both wounds contributed to the victim's death. The court agreed that the lower court' decision was proper to reject the instruction: "if you believe from the evidence that it is impossible to tell whether Will Farrell died from the wound in the throat, or the wound in the abdomen, you are bound to acquit." According to the court, the instruction assumed that death must have resulted wholly from one wound or the other, and ignored the fact that both might have contributed as the jury could have found from the evidence.

Note: Research the case to read the entire case history and complete court opinion.

QUESTIONS & NOTES

[1] Jude and his wife Janet had a terrible argument in which, Jude hit Janet with a heavy blow to the face. Janet furious entered the kitchen and came out with a knife attempting to stab Jude in the chest area. Jude reached for the gun and shot Janet in the right leg, Janet fell dropping the knife but Jude was not done, he wanted to teach her a lesson so, he decided to shoot her in the other leg, the second shot tore a major artery and Janet bled to death. Jude is now claiming he shot his wife in self-defense; is Jude guilty of any crime? What is the causal connection between the second shot and the killing? Can Jude be successfully charged with the murder of Janet? Explain your answer whether or not you think so.

Notes:

[2] Same scenario above, do you think a reasonable jury would have found Jude guilty of a homicide had Janet died from the first shot? If so, why? If not explain. Before you write your answer look at the choices below.

Had Janet died from the first shot

    (A) Jude will have a self defense claim

    (B) Jude will still be guilty of her homicide

    (C) Jude will not be guilty because Janet used a deadly weapon and attempted to stab Jude

    (D) Jude still guilty for using a gun instead of a knife to defend himself

    (E) (A) And (C) above

Notes:

[3] John made a drug deal with Ben and Akin; both felt John had cheated them and decided to pay John the "last visit." Armed with a gun each, they confronted John about the deal. An argument ensued and in the process Ben and Akin shot John once each in the leg and the chest simultaneously causing his death. Akin now claims that since evidence revealed he shot John in the leg, his shot could not have killed him but rather Ben's shot since it was to the chest. Is Akin right? Is there any causal connection between Akin's shot and the homicide? Do you think Akin and Ben are equally guilty of the homicide? Do you believe Akin's conduct proximately caused the homicide irrespective of the extent of his contribution, such that he is equally liable as Ben?

Notes:

[4] John fired a shot at Ben during a fracas between the two. Ben was rushed to the emergency as a result of injuries suffered from the shot and died 3 days later. Evidence and doctor's report indicate Ben actually died from pneumonia. Is John the cause of death? See Quinn v. State, 106 Miss. 844, 64 So. 738 (1914)

Notes:

Pablo and Riviera were drinking at a friend's party when they began to argue over Carlotta a neighborhood beauty. Pablo slapped Riviera in the face and both began to fight. Riviera pulled out a gun and shot Pablo in the chest near his heart. Pablo was rushed to the hospital, where emergency surgery was performed and the bullet was removed successfully. However, during surgery, the surgeon discovered a tumor near Pablo's heart. He attempted to remove it but Pablo died during surgery to remove the tumor.

If Riviera is charged with the murder of Pablo, his best defense is that

(A) Surgeon's action caused Pablo's death because his attempt to remove tumor did break the chain of causation
(B) He had no intent to kill Pablo
(C) He killed Pablo in the heat of passion and actual provocation
(D) Pablo would have died from the tumor despite the gun shot wound
(E) None of the above

[5] Even if physicians were negligent in believing the victim was dead before they performed a nephrectomy and even if such negligence was a contributing factor to the victim's death, the physicians' negligence does not break the chain of causation and death is still attributable to the victim being shot by the defendant. Granmore v. State, 85 Wis.2d 722, 271 N.W.2d 402 (1978)

Notes:

KIBBE V. HENDERSON

United States Court of Appeals, Second Circuit, 1976
534 F.2d 493

On the evening of December 30, 1970, Kibbe and his codefendant, Roy Krall, met the deceased, George Stafford, at a bar in Rochester, New York. Stafford had been drinking heavily and by about 9:00 p.m. he was so intoxicated that the bartender refused to serve him further. The defendants saw Stafford tender a one hundred dollar bill for payment, which the bartender refused. Later same night, Stafford asked for a ride to Canandaigua from the other patrons in the bar. Kibbe and Krall, who confessed to having already decided to rob Stafford, offered a ride and the three men left the bar together. Before leaving for Canandaigua, the three went to a second bar where the bartender at the bar also refused to serve Stafford because of his intoxicated condition. The three proceeded to a third bar, where each was served additional drinks.

Kibbe, Krall and Stafford left for Canandaigua in Kibbe's car about 9:30 that evening. Based on statements of the defendants, as Krall was driving the car, Kibbe demanded Stafford's money and, after taking it, forced Stafford to pull down his trousers and remove his boots to prove he had no more. At around 9:30 and 9:40 p.m., Stafford was abandoned on the side of an unlit, rural two-lane highway. His boots and jacket were also placed on the shoulder of the highway. Stafford's eyeglasses, however, remained in the car. Based on testimony it was "very cold" that night and that strong winds were blowing recently falling snow across the highway.

About half an hour after Kibbe and Krall had abandoned Stafford, Michael Blake, a college student, was driving his pickup truck northbound on the highway at 50 miles an hour, ten miles per hour in excess of the posted speed limit. A car passed Blake in a southbound direction and the driver flashed his headlights at Blake. Immediately thereafter, Blake saw Stafford sitting in the middle of the northbound lane with his hands in the air, Blake testified that he "went into a kind of shock" as soon as he saw Stafford, and that he did not apply his brakes. He also said that he did not attempt to avoid hitting Stafford because he "didn't have time to react." After the collision, Blake stopped his truck and attempted to help Stafford, during which he found the decedent's trousers were around his ankles and his shirt was up to his chest. Stafford had neither his jacket nor boots.

Stafford suffered massive head and body injuries as a result of the collision and died shortly thereafter. An autopsy revealed a high alcohol concentration of .25% in his blood. The medical examiner testified that these injuries were the direct cause of death.

Kibbe and Krall were apprehended on December 31, 1970. They were tried for robbery and for the murder of Stafford under New York Penal Law § 125.25(2) which provides:

A person is guilty of murder in the second degree when:

(2) Under circumstances evincing a depraved indifference to human life, he recklessly engages in conduct, which creates a great risk of death to another person and thereby causes the death of another person.

In the instruction to the jury, the judge failed to define or explain the issue of causation as the term is used in § 125.25(2). No mention was made of the legal effect of intervening or supervening cause. Nevertheless, defense counsel failed to take any exception whatsoever to this omission. The jury returned guilty verdicts on the charges of second-degree murder, second-degree robbery, and third degree grand larceny. Kibbe was sentenced to concurrent terms of imprisonment of 15 years to life on the murder conviction, 5 to 15 years on the robbery conviction, and up to 4 years on the grand larceny conviction.

The Appellate Division affirmed the conviction on finding that there was enough evidence that Stafford's death was caused by appellant's acts including the acts of Blake. Kibbe then petitioned for habeas corpus in the District Court for the Northern District. Judge Foley denied the petition and, on the question of the jury charge and noted that the correctness of the instructions does not raise a constitutional claim cognizable in habeas corpus. Kibbe then, filed an appeal.

In conclusion, the court of appeals, found that the appellant was denied of due process because the jury was not adequately instructed in order to make a finding beyond a reasonable doubt. The court stated that If the jury had been made aware of the proper legal standards, the evidence, if believed, could have injected an element of reasonable doubt into the jury's deliberations as to whether defendants foresaw or could have foreseen that about one-half hour after they abandoned Stafford, he would be struck in the middle of a highway by the driver of a speeding truck, who failed to react in such a way to avoid collision. Therefore, the incomplete instruction was instrumental in the decision to deny appellant of his rights to due process.

Note: Please research the case for the complete case history and court deliberations.

QUESTIONS

[1] Based on the decision of the court, do you agree that failure of the trial judge to give proper instruction, weigh heavily on the final judgment, though, the appellant could have known the victim was prone to any form of misfortune, when he was abandoned? Please explain, a Yes or No answer is not enough. Utilize space provided below for your response.

Notes:

[2] Consider the following scenario **A** burglarized the home of **B**, murdered **B** and stole her jewelries. One day after the burglary and murder of **B**, **C B**'s daughter arrived to pay her mother a visit. On learning of her mother's death, **C** collapsed and was pronounced dead at the hospital. Evidence and autopsy report show **C** died from a complicated heart failure. Medical records also indicate **C** had suffered a stroke twice before. Based on these facts, can **A** be properly charged for the murder of **C**? If so, how? If not explain.

Notes:

In question (2) above what happens to defendant (A)

(A) A can be charged with the murder of C because "but" for his action and burglary C would not have died

(B) A cannot be charged with the murder of C because his action was too remote to cause C's death

(C) A can be charge because his action is the proximate cause of C's death

(D) A can be charged because death of B complicated C's heart problem

(E) A cannot be charged because C's complicated heart failure caused C's death

(F) (B) And (E) above

[3] Same scenario but with a little change, **A** had just finished both burglary and murder of **B** and was about to leave the home when **C** arrived suddenly; **A** while attempting to leave the house collided with **C,** shoved her aside, and escaped. The impact and sudden shock from the sight of **A,** made **C** collapse and die. All evidence, medical records and autopsy show same as above. **A** has been charged with the murder of **C**; is **A** the cause of death? If so, how? If not, explain below.

Notes:

[4] As a result of a drug dealing gone wrong, George shoots Michael causing Michael to flee. Michael realized it was not a serious wound and chose to hide in the bushes under a tree to avoid being shot twice by George. Unbeknownst, another drug dealing was ongoing nearby, Sam the drug dealer saw Michael and thinking he was being arrested, shoots at him in order to escape. Michael later died from his wounds. Based on these facts, who is guilty of murder? George claims he did not cause Michael's death, is he right? Applying the theories of causation, do you think both caused Michael's death? To answer these questions please apply the theories of causation stated at the beginning of this chapter.

Note: *Sometimes, an intervening act can be a response to the initial actions of the defendant when it involves a reaction to the conditions created by the defendant.*

Notes:

[5] Do you think the instructions given by the trial judge in *Kibbe* is sufficient enough to find defendants guilty, based on the argument that the jury was made aware that defendants' conduct, was the cause of death even though, it may not have been the only cause?

Notes:

While waiting at a bus stop in front of his home, Bob was struck in the chest by a stray bullet from a drug dealing gone bad. The shooter Abel continued to pursue his intended victim without knowledge he had shot Bob. Two days before the incident, Jeff, a business partner of Bob had planned to murder Bob for cheating him out of a business deal. Jeff had purchased a gun a day earlier and on the night of the shooting, he was on his way to carry out his plan. As Jeff approached Bob's house, he saw him holding his chest but it was too dark to see he was bleeding from the earlier shooting. Jeff opened fire instantly and killed Bob. Evidence revealed the stray bullet was not life threatening.

Who is responsible for the murder of Bob?

(A) Abel is responsible because he shot Bob first

(B) Abel and Jeff are equally responsible for the murder of Bob

(C) Jeff killed Bob because he premeditated Bob's murder and carried out his plan

(D) Abel killed Bob because Abel is a drug dealer who failed to take reasonable care

(E) None of the above

[6] Is it sound argument to claim the omission of proper instruction as in *Kibbe*, substantially affected the jury deliberations in finding defendants guilty?

Notes:

Michael, intending to kill Ferdinand, bought a manual on bomb making. He constructed a bomb and placed the device in Ferdinand's car knowing he had a long trip ahead following day. Michael timed the bomb to explode one hour after takeoff. Barely 30 minutes to his trip, a Hummer that ran through a red light struck Ferdinand's car, killing Ferdinand instantly. Evidence show the collision deactivated the explosive, which failed to go off.

If prosecuted for murder, Michael should be found

(A) Guilty, because Ferdinand would have been killed had the bomb exploded

(B) Guilty, because Michael premeditated Ferdinand's death before the accident

(C) Guilty, Michael was only lucky the bomb did not go off

(D) Not guilty, because Michael did not cause Ferdinand's death

(E) (B) And (D) above

[7] Based on facts of the *Kibbe* case, do you believe the defendants should have known Stafford was prone to being hit by a truck? Is it proper to conclude the events that ensued were foreseeable enough to remove the need for a due process consideration? Write a one-page essay below showing your understanding of the case.

Notes:

STATE V. SAUTER

Supreme Court of Arizona, In Banc, 1978
120 Ariz. 222, 585 P.2d. 242

After a trial by jury, the appellant Richard Robert Sauter, was convicted of voluntary manslaughter, and appeals.

While intoxicated and during the course of an altercation, the appellant stabbed Matt Charles Lines. Lines, was transported to the emergency room of a hospital in Phoenix, Arizona, where he was attended by a general surgeon. The surgeon opened the abdominal cavity and repaired lacerations to the anterior and posterior stomach walls, the main stomach artery, the superior pancreatic artery and pancreatic tissue. The surgeon also palpitated the abdominal aorta, but did not observe bleeding in the area. After the surgery, Lines continued to loose large amounts of blood. An autopsy revealed that he died from the loss of blood, principally through a one-inch, unrepaired laceration in the abdominal aorta.

Appellant claimed that he was guilty of assault and not homicide because of the intervening malpractice of the surgeon who failed to discover the laceration in Lines' aorta, and said that error occurred when the trial court refused to allow evidence of the surgeon's failure to discover the wound to Lines' aorta.

The court rejected appellant's arguments and affirmed the conviction, based on the principle that, where a person causes upon another a wound, which is dangerous and calculated to endanger or destroy life, it is no defense to a charge of homicide that the victim's death was a result of, unskillful or improper treatment of the wound or injury by the physicians or surgeons. The intervention of the medical malpractice will only constitute a defense, if victim's death was not induced at all by the original wound.

Note: Find the case State v. Sauter, for a complete case history and court' opinion.

NOTES

In 2011 Dr. Conrad Murray, Michael Jackson's physician, was charged with involuntary manslaughter in the death of the pop icon. He was eventually found guilty of the negligent homicide of Mr. Jackson.

Followings are my analysis of the case and its applicability to the theory of causation taken from a blog I wrote about the case on November 8, 2011.

As Dr. Conrad Murray is hurled to jail to await sentencing after jury's verdict, that found him guilty of involuntary manslaughter, many wonder what actually led the jury to arrive at such a decision after weeks of deliberation and tons of evidence scrutiny. Recently, I wrote an article on the case titled *"Involuntary Manslaughter: Meaning of the Charge in re Michael Jackson."* The article generated a lot of interests among those interested in knowing the meaning of *involuntary manslaughter*. However, in this case, I have decided to explain what may have led the jury to arrive at a guilty verdict.

To a non-legal mind, a guilty verdict in the Michael Jackson's case, look rather trivial or mundane but nonetheless, every decision by the court or the jury must be supported by evidence and all elements of the charge must be established to arrive at a satisfied verdict. The crime of involuntary manslaughter or negligent homicide is defined in such a way that the result of a conduct is required before its commission can be established. Therefore, the answer to how the jury arrived at a guilty verdict in the Jackson' case, can be found in the legal theory of **causation**.

From the tort theory of negligence we learn that besides proving duty and breach of duty, the prosecution must also establish proximate cause. It must show that the defendant's action or omission is the legal cause of injury suffered by the victim. Likewise, in criminal law we must find a causal connection between the act and the harmful result. In any civilized criminal justice, liability cannot be enforced on a defendant unless it is determined the action punished, is in some degree a result of his act. Imagine one charged with murder and sentenced to life imprisonment when all evidence shows that his action did not cause the victim's death. In fact, it is fair to say that such a sentence is far from proper justice. The issue is not what people say is the cause but rather what the law says is the cause of the victim's demise.

In the Michael Jackson case, to find Dr. Murray guilty as concluded the jury must have looked through all evidence including testimonies. Based on such evidence it came to the conclusion that Dr. Murray indeed *caused* Mr. Jackson's death. "It has been said that an act which in no way contributed to the result in question cannot be a cause of it. This of course, does not mean that an event, which *might* have happened in the same way though the defendant's act or omission had not occurred, is not a result of it. The question is not what would have happened, but what did happen." (See Beale, *The Proximate Consequences of An Act*, 33 Harv.Law Rev 633, 638 (1920))

In criminal negligence cases such as this, what is important is that whenever a crime demands the occurrence of a specific conduct for its commission, it is essential that the defendant's conduct is the "legal or proximate" cause of the result in order for a guilty verdict to stand or else no culpability can be established. For example, the crime of *homicide* (unlawful killing of a human being), requires the death of a person therefore, defendant's action or omission must be the legal cause of death to establish guiltiness. This is to say that 'but for' defendant's action or omission, the result (death) would not have occurred.

In the Michael Jackson case, the jury was able to conclude by clear and convincing evidence that Dr. Murray's negligent action in giving Mr. Jackson an illegal dose of propofol is both proximate and legal cause of the pop icon's death. This means that 'but for' Dr. Murray's negligent act of giving Mr. Jackson propofol, Mr. Jackson would not have died.

"A primary requisite to either criminal or civil liability is that the act of the defendant be the cause in fact of the injury. This requirement is embodied in the familiar *causa sine qua non* rule, generally called the 'but for' rule. This test generally is satisfactory when applied in negative form, and it is a basic principle that a defendant is not liable unless the injury would not have resulted but for his wrongful act. But as an affirmative test the 'but for' rule provides no infallible standard and does not constitute a fair test of liability in the absence of further qualification. ...

"The modern authorities, while agreed that the 'but for' test is inadequate differ materially in their concepts of proximate causation. The theories conveniently may be placed in two groups. One group seeks the necessary connection between the result and the act; the other, between the result and the actor's mind." (**See Focht,** *Proximate Cause in the Law of Homicide-With Special Reference to California Cases,* **12 So.Cal.L.Rev. 19, 20-21 (1938))**

To establish proximate cause three tests are required: Intention, probability, and the absence of an independent-intervening force. "Any intended consequence of an act is proximate. There is no doubt that Dr. Murray intended to give Mr. Jackson propofol. Even though, he had no intent to kill, Dr. Murray knows or should have known that improper application of propofol would cause death. As a man of adequate intelligence with proper medical training, he is expected to know the adverse effects of illegal administration of propofol. "It would plainly be absurd that a person should be allowed to act with an intention to produce a certain consequence, and then when that very consequence in fact follows his act, to escape liability for it on the plea that it was not proximate". (**See Terry,** *Proximate Consequences in the Law of Torts,* **28 Harv.L.10, 17-20**

(1914)) Based on this, the required intent to establish causation can be easily inferred, meaning Dr. Murray intended a negligent act that caused the homicide.

Probability is a name for someone's opinion or guess as to whether a consequence will result. To establish that the actor knows the probable consequence of his action, it is important the person whose opinion is taken, is a reasonable and prudent man in the situation of the actor. There is no doubt death is a foreseeable consequence of illegal administration of propofol to a human being. A reasonable and prudent physician in the position of Dr. Murray would known that death is a foreseeable consequence of negligent administration of propofol in a home setting. Anesthesiologists use propofol for surgery and not as a sleeping agent; Dr. Murray knew or should have known the probable and foreseeable consequence of his actions when he administered the drug.

The third test of proximateness is the non-intervention of an independent cause between the original cause and the consequence in question. Therefore, it is proper to call it an isolating cause. To establish his negligent act did not cause Mr. Jackson's death, Dr. Murray would have to show something else happened in the form of an independent force that caused death. Here, Dr. Murray claims the pop icon, injected himself with the propofol that caused his death. He claims that self-administration of propofol is the independent force that caused death.

Normally, in negligent cases, prove of a separate intervening force as the cause of death may exculpate the defendant or make him partially liable. Even in such cases, the foreign force must be equal to the defendant's action to share liability but if the intervening force is a dominant force, the defendant will not be culpable. Nonetheless, the defendant must still show that he did not set in motion the events that led to victim's death. Dr. Murray failed to prove Mr. Jackson injected himself with propofol, and even if he could prove so, facts will show that but for the negligent act of Dr. Murray, Mr. Jackson would not have access to propofol.

All evidence point to the fact that no independent or intervening force caused Mr. Jackson's death but the negligent act of Dr. Murray, in providing him with a drug he should not have had. These facts establish the third requirement needed to prove causation.

A guilty verdict means, defendant would spend few years in jail; however, he may still face a civil law suit. If guilty as in the case of Dr. Murray, a defendant would be asked to pay damages to the estate of the deceased. Physicians have medical malpractice insurance and in most cases, the insurance pays the fine to a substantial limit.

For such a defendant, the practice of medicine could be over. Medical Board of the states where defendant is licensed to practice determines whether he gets his license back.[47]

---

[47] Adeyemi Oshunrinade, **LEGAL THEORY OF CAUSATION**: *Why Guilty, Dr. Murray in re Michael Jackson* at http://san0670.com

Dr. Murray was eventually sentenced to four years in jail and at the time of writing, he was considering appealing his conviction but later released after serving his term.

Chapter Eight

Mens Rea

Intent

Crime is known to require both act and intent; the term *mens rea* is used in criminal law to denote "criminal responsibility" and thus means answerability to the criminal law. After all, no one should be answerable to the criminal law for crime not legally committed by him for to do so, is a miscarriage of justice. The issue of mens rea as it applies in criminal law, often comes into place when in connection with consequences attributable to the accused within the rules of imputability. The fact that one is charged with a crime and sentenced does not mean the accused is answerable to the crime. Crime requires both act and intent; therefore, one who acts without the intent to achieve the end result may be exculpated for lack of the required mens rea to commit the crime.

The term "intent" as is in criminal law is different from "intention." To establish guiltiness in criminal law, there must be a union or joint operation of both *act* and *intent*. In essence, to be guilty and responsible for a crime, the accused must be blameworthy. In the early days of the development of Common Law Crimes, judges have declared some conduct to be criminal even though, such conduct lack the required state of mind. Meaning the accused is made to pay for the action even when the *bad* or *evil* state of mind required is missing.

Since the 1600s, the judges have defined common law crimes to include besides the prescribed action or omission some prescribed bad or evil state of mind. The basic premise is that for criminal liability to stand, some *mens rea* is required. This notion is expressed by the Latin Maxim *actus not facit reum nisi mens sit rea*, meaning [*an act does not make one guilty unless his mind is guilty*]. Some words and phrases are used by judges to express the required state of mind necessary, to commit a crime. Such phrases include *"maliciously"* [as in the cases of murder, arson, and criminal mischief], *"fraudulently"* [as in cases of forgery], *"feloniously"* [as in the crime of larceny], *"willfully"* [usually in perjury cases], and *"with intent"* [as with intent to commit a robbery or with intent to steal].

Most crimes today are statutory crimes and most jurisdictions of the United States have abolished the common law and have stated the common law crimes in the form of statutory laws. Since every crime is made up of both the *physical part* and the *mental part*, both parts must act in concord for the defendant to be blameworthy and the union of both parts is required for conviction of crime. The *guilty deed* must be in agreement with the *guilty mind* to be blameworthy.

If the prosecution can prove the existence of the physical part of the crime charged, and that this action is attributable to the defendant within the legal rules of imputability, then the prosecution has established his *actus reus*. Also if the prosecution can prove that in doing what he did the defendant's state of mind was one which satisfies the requirements of the mental element of the crime charged, then his *mens rea* has been established. The combination of both as a unit constitutes criminal guilt.

The mental element of a crime is sometimes referred to as a [*general state of mind*] common to all crimes. However, additional mental element may be required for some specific crimes. For example, a 7-year-old who commits murder may be too young to have the state of mind or mental element required for the crime of murder and therefore, not blameworthy. This means that for *mens rea*, the mind of the individual must not be too young. Also for *mens rea* purposes, the defendant must have a complete state of mind for one with a diminished capacity or with a greatly disturbed faculty may lack the required state of mind and therefore, not blameworthy as charged.

To establish the required *mens rea*, every mental pattern, which contains any factor sufficient in law to exculpate the defendant, must be excluded or else the defendant lacks the required state of mind to commit the crime. If after exclusion of such factors the required intent to commit the offense is found to be present, then the case is that of a *"general mens rea."* For some crimes, criminal *negligence* may be substituted for the required intent to commit the offense.

In essence to establish *mens rea*, there must be lacking any factor sufficient enough to exculpate the defendant. Besides this requirement, there must also be the intent to do the deed known as the *actus reus* of the offense charged; or else, there must be some other mental state recognized as substitute such as *criminal negligence* as earlier indicated.

Once the *mens rea* and the *actus reus* are established, the defendant is said to possess the *"general intent"* or the *"general criminal intent"* common to all crimes. This is sufficient to establish guiltiness such that the defendant is blameworthy for the proscribed crime. The *actus reus* required for one crime differs from another; for example, the crime of burglary requires that the defendant *break* into the *dwelling* of *another* at *night*; for the crime of murder, the *actus reus* is *homicide* known as the unlawful killing of another with malice aforethought, meaning that for the defendant to commit the crime of murder, a homicide must have taken place.

On the other hand, the *mens rea* required for a Common-law burglary is the *intent* to commit a felony; and for the crime of battery no more is required than the *"general intent"* which may be substituted with criminal negligence. To determine the establishment of *mens rea* it is essential to see the state of mind of the defendant as well as the crime with which he is charged. Also important is that the *actus reus* and the *mens rea* must act in concord to find the defendant guilty.

LIMICY V. STATE

Court of Criminal Appeals of Texas, 1945
148 Tex.Cr.R. 130, 185 S.W.2d 571

The defendant sentenced to four years for committing an abortion, appealed. The charge alleges that John Limicy willfully and designedly committed an assault upon Lula May Howard, a pregnant woman. He also unlawfully, and designedly caused Lula May Howard, to have an abortion by striking, kicking, beating and violently using Lula May Howard, during her pregnancy.

The charge claimed that appellant "designedly" committed the offense, with the intention to force an abortion. The principal question raised by the appeal is on the sufficiency of the evidence to support a finding in accordance with the indictment.

The prosecuting Witness Lula May Howard, was a twenty-year-old girl, who lived with appellant since 1940, both were not married. They had a child out of wedlock and she had a miscarriage at a previous time. Some five months before the date of the alleged crime they had discovered that she was again pregnant and this fact was frequently discussed between them.

Based on prosecutor's account, the fight between her and the appellant began on July 8th. He first beat her with a chair. That was during the nighttime. After she succeeded in getting the chair away from him he grabbed a rub board and broke it over her head. He also broke the broom handle in striking her. ... They fussed and fought intermittently until Monday, July 10, following the Saturday night when she describes the fight as beginning. At the end of the fighting, she suffered wounds on her shoulders and head. A doctor was called during the night. The next day Dr. Wilson testified in the case that in his opinion the premature birth of the child, after it had died in the mother's wound, was brought about by the injuries, which he found inflicted on the prosecutrix.

In its final ruling, the court reversed the conviction and remanded the case, because there was no evidence supporting the conclusion reached by the jury of intent to commit an abortion. Though, Intent may be presumed from all of the facts and circumstances of a case, the court found that, mere fact of the premature birth of the child as a result of the things done, considered with all of the circumstances of the case, does not suffice to establish intent and justifiable conviction. The fact that the prosecutrix took an active part and possibly the lead in the fight was in consideration. If he originated the fight without cause support would've been given to the State's argument.

Note: Find the case using the case number above for the entire court opinion and case history.

NOTES AND QUESTIONS

[1] Consider the following scenario; the defendant threw a stone at some persons with whom he had been fighting. The intention, was to strike one or more of those persons however, the stone passed over their heads and broke a large plate glass window. Based on the facts, can the defendant be guilty of a misdemeanor for "unlawfully" and "maliciously" causing damage to a personal property? See *Pembliton (1984) L.R. 2 C.C.R. 119.*

Notes:

[2] Based on the same scenario above, can you conclude for a fact that the defendant willfully and intentionally committed the result as stated? Can he be liable as charged considering the intent requirement for the crime in this case?

Notes:

Brittany worked as a nurse in the intensive care unit of Carlisle Hospital. She was assigned to care for Bruce a rheumatism patient languishing in pain and about to die. Brittany discussed Bruce's case with the attending physicians and all told Brittany there was nothing they could do to save Bruce's life than to keep him on a life support to aid his breathing for a month, when he is expected to die. Distraught, Brittany went into Bruce's room one night and saw the cleaning lady unintentional disconnect Bruce's breathing machine with a mop. After the cleaning lady left unaware of what transpired, Brittany watched and did nothing as Bruce struggled to breath. Bruce died same night because he could not breath.

If Brittany is charged with the murder of Bruce, she should be:

(A) Acquitted, because Bruce was going to die anyway

(B) Acquitted, because she only has a moral duty to help Bruce

(C) Convicted, because as a nurse professional placed in Bruce's care, she had an affirmative duty of care to save Bruce's life

(D) Convicted, because she showed lack of compassion for Bruce

(E) (C) And (D) above

[3] Assume the jury found based on evidence that the defendant committed the act recklessly, knowing there was a window near, which the stone might probably hit. Would that be enough to convict the defendant for damaging a personal property?

Notes:

[4] Think about the argument that the defendant threw the stone intending it to strike only the people he was fighting with and not intending to break the window; is this sufficient enough to exculpate him?

Notes:

[5] Ibrahim entered the house of Michael with the intention to steal his gold necklace, he lighted a match to get a better view of the jewelry box but this ignited the floor and the house completely burnt down. Facts show that Michael had earlier mistakenly spilled some gasoline on the floor, which he did not clean properly before the incident. Can Ibrahim be maliciously liable for setting the house on fire?

Based on question (5) above Ibrahim is:

    (A) Liable, for intending to burn the house down

    (B) Not liable, because he only came to steal

    (C) Liable, for setting in motion the events that led to burning the house

    (D) Not liable, because Michael spilled gasoline on floor

    (E) None of the above

Notes:

[6] In *Faulkner (1877) 13 Cox 550*, the defendant a sailor, went into the hold of a ship to steal some rum. In the process, he lit a match to have a better view, but this ignited the rum causing a fire that destroyed the entire ship. The defendant was convicted by the jury of violating the Malicious Damage Act for maliciously setting fire to the ship. The court, per Barry, J., reversed: "The jury were in fact, directed to give a verdict of guilty upon the simple ground that the firing of the ship, though accidental, was caused by an act done in the course of, or immediately consequent upon, a felonious operation, and no question of the prisoner's malice, constructive or otherwise, was left to the jury. I am of opinion that, according to *Reg. v. Pembliton,* that direction was erroneous, and that the conviction should be quashed."

Notes:

[7] In *State v. Harley, 72 N.M. 377, 384 P.2d 252 (1963)*, the defendant was found guilty and convicted of *mayhem*. Defendant claimed that though, he struck the blow, which put out the victim's eye, there was no proof he intended to maim the victim and that the harm was as a result of the victim turning his head at the moment of the blow. The court disagreed and affirmed, because the conduct of the appellant falls well within the rules so as to make him liable for the consequences of an unlawful act, even though, such consequences may not have been intended. The principle is that, one who in the commission of a wrongful act, commits another wrong not meant by him, is nevertheless liable for the latter wrong. According to the court, the appellant deliberately committed the crime of assault and battery, and in so doing committed mayhem.

Notes:

SMALLWOOD V. STATE

Maryland Court of Appeals
343 Md. 97, 680 A.2d 512 (1996)

In the case, the court was called to examine the use of circumstantial evidence to infer that a defendant possessed the intent to kill needed for a conviction of attempted murder or assault with intent to murder. We conclude that such an inference is not supportable under the facts of this case.

On August 29, 1991, Dwight Ralph Smallwood was found infected with Human Immunodeficiency Virus (HIV). Based on medical records from the Prince George's County Detention Center, he was informed of his HIV-positive status by September 21, 1991. In February 1992, a social worker informed Smallwood of the necessity of practicing "safe sex" to avoid transmitting the virus to his sexual partners, and in July 1993, Smallwood told health care providers at Children's Hospital that he had only one sexual partner and that they always used condoms. Smallwood again tested positive to HIV in February and March of 1994.

On September 26, 1993, Smallwood and an accomplice robbed a woman at gunpoint, and forced her into a grove of trees where each man alternately placed a gun to her head while the other one raped her. On September 28, 1993, Smallwood and an accomplice robbed a second woman at gunpoint and took her to a secluded location, where Smallwood inserted his penis into her with "slight penetration." On September 30, 1993, Smallwood and an accomplice robbed yet a third woman, also at gunpoint, and took her to a local school where she was forced to perform oral sex on Smallwood and was raped by him. In each of these episodes, Smallwood threatened to kill his victims if they did not cooperate or to return and shoot them if they reported his crimes. Smallwood did not wear a condom during any of these criminal episodes.

Based on his attack on September 28, 1993, Smallwood was charged with, among other crimes, attempted first-degree rape, robbery with deadly weapon, assault with intent to murder, and reckless endangerment. In separate indictments, Smallwood was also charged with the attempted second-degree murder of each of his three victims. On October 11, 1994, Smallwood pled guilty in the Circuit Court for Prince George's County to attempted first-degree rape and robbery with a deadly weapon. The Circuit Court also convicted Smallwood of assault with intent to murder and reckless endangerment based upon his September 28, 1993 attack, and convicted Smallwood of all three counts of attempted second-degree murder.

Following the conviction, Smallwood was sentenced to concurrent sentences of life imprisonment for attempted rape, twenty years imprisonment for robbery with a deadly weapon, thirty years imprisonment for assault with intent to murder, and five years imprisonment for reckless endangerment. The Circuit Court also imposed a concurrent thirty-year sentence for each of the three counts of attempted second-degree murder. The Circuit Court's judgments were affirmed in part and reversed in part by the Court of Special Appeals [, which] found that the evidence was sufficient for the Trial Court to conclude that Smallwood intended to kill his victims and upheld all of his convictions. Smallwood appealed and the court granted Certiorari to consider whether the Trial Court could properly conclude that Smallwood possessed the requisite intent to support his convictions of attempted second-degree murder and assault with intent to murder.

Smallwood asserts that the Trial Court lacked enough evidence to support its conclusion that he intended to kill his three victims. Smallwood argues that the fact that he engaged in unprotected sexual intercourse, even though he knew that he carried HIV, is insufficient to infer an intent to kill. The most that can reasonably be inferred, Smallwood contends, is that he is guilty of recklessly endangering his victims by exposing them to the risk that they would become infected themselves.

In conclusion, the court reversed Smallwood's convictions for attempted murder and assault with intent to commit murder, based on its findings that while the risk to which Smallwood exposed his victims when he forced them to engage in unprotected sexual activity must not be minimized, the State has shown no evidence from which to establish that death by AIDS is a probable result of Smallwood's actions. There was also no additional evidence from which to infer the intent to kill. Smallwood's actions showed intent to commit rape and armed robbery, the crimes for which he pled guilty. Therefore, the court found no evidence of Smallwood's intent to kill.

Note: Please research the case for the entire case background and court opinion.

NOTES AND QUESTIONS

[1] Looking at the court's ruling in *Smallwood*, do you agree with the opinion that the defendant did not intend the death of his victims? Consider the fact that even though, Smallwood attacked each of the victims once, he did in fact attacked three different women on three separate occasions. Is it logical to conclude based on such evidence, that the defendant Smallwood, acted with intent? Discuss your answer below with reference to *Smallwood*.

Notes:

[2] Many States now have laws making it illegal for anyone to knowingly transmit or expose another individual to HIV. Based on such laws, is it proper to conclude that defendants without knowledge of their HIV status should escape prosecution and penalty?

Notes:

Aware that he had HIV Simmons continued to sleep with women unprotected. In fact, he told his closest friend he would pass the disease to every woman unfortunate to be intimate with him. Simmons had a lot of charms and can easily win a woman over. He met Stephanie a formal beauty queen. After about a year dating Stephanie found out she had contracted HIV, she could not bear the stigma and suffered a huge depression caused by rejection. Five years later, Stephanie died from a serious illness. Tests indicated her immune was weakened due to HIV and she could not fight the disease.

Stephanie's parents have sued, of what crime is Simmons guilty?

(A) Murder for knowingly infecting Stephanie

(B) Voluntary manslaughter

(C) Involuntary manslaughter

(D) Sexual battery

(E) Rape for sleeping with Stephanie knowing he had HIV

(F) None of the above

[3] ***General and Specific Intent***: The loose phrases "criminal intent" and "general intent" has not made courts to miss the fact that "intent" in the proper sense, has the same meaning as "intention." However, in most cases, courts have interpreted intent to denote purpose or design. Sometimes, "general intent" is used in the same way as "criminal intent" or it may be used to indicate all forms of mental state required for an act. "General intent" may also be substituted for the intent to do an act on an undetermined occasion, while "specific intent" may denote the intent to do an act at a particular time and place; or it may be limited to the one mental state of intent. The attempt to define or assign meaning to the term "intent" has not been without difficulties in criminal law. Some writers in the field, tried to assign meaning to the term by defining "intention" as "the attitude of the mind in which the doer of an act adverts to a consequence of the act and desires it to follow. But the doer of an act may advert to a consequence and not desire it: and therefore not intend it."[48]

Other writers have expressed that a result is intended only if it is contemplated as a probable consequence whether it is desired or not.[49] Others such as Salmond require the element of desire but give it a somewhat forced construction. According to Salmond, 'a man desires not only the end but also the means to the end, and hence desires, although he may "deeply regret" the necessity for, the means'.[50] In dealing with cases involving intention, more is required than an expectation that the consequence is likely to result from the act. Put another way, it is not necessary that the consequence be desired though, the element may become important. One, who acts for the purpose of causing a result, intends that result whether it is likely to materialize or not. On the other hand, he intends the consequence, which he knows would be the result of his act whether he desires it, regrets it or indifferent as to it.

The most common application of "specific intent" is the requirement of a specified intention, a special mental element with respect to the *actus reus of the crime*. For example, the physical part of the crime of larceny is the taking and the carrying away of the personal property of another. However, these acts may be done intentionally, deliberately, with full knowledge of all the facts and complete understanding of the wrongfulness of the act without constituting larceny. Therefore, in addition to the mental element requirement i.e. the *taking* and *carrying* away of the property, it must also be established that the defendant "intended to steal" the property. A defendant may take and carry away the property of another, with the desire to use and return it

---

[48] Markby, *Elements of Law, § 220 (4ᵗʰ ed. 1989)*
[49] Austin, *Jurisprudence 424 (5ᵗʰ ed. 1885)*
[50] Rollin M. Perkins et al, *Criminal Law and Procedure supra, (6ᵗʰ ed. 1984) P. 472: in ref. Salmond, Jurisprudence 395 (8 ed. 1930)*

so, if this unauthorized use of property is done with the intention of returning it, then the state of mind required for the crime of larceny is lacking. Such a defendant may not be criminally liable for larceny but liable only in a civil suit for unauthorized or misuse of property only. For a defendant to be liable criminally under common law larceny he must not only take and carry away other's property by trespass, there must be an additional state of mind, the requisite "intent" to steal.

Likewise, common law burglary demands a breaking and entry into the dwelling of another. The crime may not be defined as the breaking and entry into the dwelling of another in the "nighttime," because this can be done without committing the felony. Therefore, in addition to the mental state required for burglary, it must also be established that the defendant acted "with intent to commit a felony;" meaning that to be criminally liable for common law burglary, the defendant in addition to breaking and entering the dwelling at nighttime, must intend to commit a felony. This additional requirement is a "specific intent," necessary to establish guilt of the crime of burglary.

Notes:

George purchased a vicious Pit-bull to protect his guitar store after suffering several break-ins. The dog was specifically trained to attack intruders and cause serious injury if necessary. Dave and Sam two neighborhood Teens broke into the store with the intention to play with the guitars and then leave. In fact, Dave told his girlfriend of their intentions before leaving home on the night in question. Both were attacked and killed by George's Pit-bull as they entered the store. Their bodies were found badly mutilated the following morning.

Both parents have sued George for the boys' deaths.

Of what crime is George guilty?

- (A) Murder for creating a situation with a risk that the intruder may die or suffer serious bodily injury
- (B) Voluntary manslaughter
- (C) Depraved-heart murder for showing a reckless disregard for human life
- (D) Involuntary manslaughter
- (E) Battery
- (F) (A) And (C) above

Chapter Nine
Homicide Defenses

Immaturity

As part of the consideration for fair justice, it is essential for the judicial system to recognize criminal incapacity based on immaturity and infancy. For the justice system to serve its purpose there must be criteria for finding one culpable and liable for a criminal act. To find a child criminally culpable for a crime requiring a mental state, which normally exists at maturity, signifies a delivery of justice too harsh. Irrespective of the harm caused by one of tender age, there must be other ways for the administration of justice besides that established for criminal prosecution.

At common law, attention was focused on two ages: a child under the age of seven is thought to have no criminal capacity. It is presumed that one of such age is incapable of a criminal act. There is an irrebuttable presumption of incapacity on the part of one so young. Also, one who has reached the age of fourteen has criminal capacity unless incapacity is proved based on other legally applicable grounds such as insanity. In essence, this means the physical age and not mental age. Between the ages of seven and fourteen, there is a rebuttable presumption of criminal incapacity, a child between these ages may be found liable only when it is proven and established that there is a clear and real appreciation of the wrongfulness of the act or conduct.

The common law of England in some instances, privilege one under the age of twenty one as to minor misdemeanors so as to escape fine, imprisonment and other serious penalties. But where a notorious crime is committed such as battery, aggravated assault, and the like which infants when full grown are as liable as others to commit, for such crimes, one above the age of fourteen, would be found equally liable to suffer as a person of age twenty-one. In some cases, the law will look at the consciousness of the guilt and discretion to determine between good and evil, in deciding whether the defense of infancy or incapacity is proper in the case. However, when it comes to serious crimes, the law has been careful in choosing the degrees of age to be exculpated or subject to criminal sanction. For example, homicide by a boy of ten was held not to be murder on the ground that one of his age, was not shown to possess the mens rea needed for murder.[51] On the other hand, a 13-year-old boy was convicted of murder in the second degree, and in affirming the conviction, the court reiterated that "Poole hid the murder weapon as well as other pieces of evidence; he fabricated stories in attempting to establish an alibi and claimed the shooting had been accidental. He testified that he knew killing people was wrong, and there was ample evidence that Poole knew the wrongfulness of his act."[52]

In such cases however, the evidence of malice required to provide age must be strong and clear beyond reasonable doubt, for criminal liability to stand or be recognized. The age of complete criminal incapacity varies according to statute and the applicable jurisdiction in the United States. Some statutes have incorporated the common law rule that children under the age of fourteen are incapable of a crime, in the absence of clear proof that at the time of the crime, they knew its wrongfulness. Others have abolished the common law rule as to the capacity of a 14-year-old, leaving the presumption of incapacity to apply only to children under the age of seven. Except for cases where the age for capacity is raised by statute. It has always been possible in legal theory to rebut the presumption of incapacity, of a 7-year-old though, the cases are rare.

In rape cases for example, common law does not allow one under the age of fourteen, to be found capable of such crime. A boy under the age of fourteen is presumed to lack the capacity for the crime of rape. 'Where two indictments were found against a 13-year-old boy, one of rape and the other of murder, the prosecution of the rape case would be stopped once the age of incapacity is established. However, the murder case would proceed with an instruction on the prima facie presumption of incapacity of a child under the age of fourteen to commit such crime'.[53] As earlier indicated, the age of capacity has been established according to statute in different jurisdictions of the United States, based on the principle that no one shall be deprived of life by reason of an act, done before reaching a specified age, to be determined by the law of each jurisdiction. This responsibility has been assumed by the Juvenile Delinquency Statutes of each jurisdiction according to state. In the recent years, there has been changes to the procedure of juvenile justice for example, some statutes provide that what is considered a crime, if committed by an adult of legal age, is not a crime but a misbehavior known as "Juvenile Delinquency" if perpetrated by a "Juvenile."

---

[51] State in Interest of S.H., *61 N.J. 108, 293 A.2d 181 (1972)*
[52] Poole v. State, *97 Nev. 175, 625 P.2d 1163, 1165 (1981)*
[53] Rollin M. Perkins et al, Criminal *Law* and Procedure (1984); P. 565

There are many factors to be considered in finding culpability for criminal offenses, most especially in homicide cases. The age of one charged may stand as a defense, based on incapacity and lack of required mental state, even though, he may have committed the most outrageous crime such as taking a human life. However, the available statute and the circumstances of each case will determine the direction of justice.

PEOPLE V. ROPER

Court of Appeals of New York
259 N.Y. 170, 181 N.E. 88 (1932)

A little before two o'clock in the morning of January 20th, 1981, two youths, with handkerchiefs covering their faces and harmed with pistols, entered a negro restaurant on Seventh avenue in New York City. At the point of the pistol, one of them compelled the people in the restaurant to go to the rear and took some money from them. The same youth shot and killed William Groce, a customer of the restaurant. The other bandit took money from the cash register. Then both escaped. ...

The question in the case was whether the jury's finding of guilt on these issues supports the defendant's conviction of the crime of murder in the first degree.

At the time of the crime, the defendant Louis Roper was between fifteen and sixteen years of age. Testimony that the defendant was under the age of sixteen was undisputed. The case was tried and submitted to the jury upon the assumption that the fact that the defendant was at the time of the homicide under the age of sixteen carries no legal consequences in a trial for murder in the first degree. The question was put before the court, to test the validity of that assumption in this case.

The court reversed the conviction. Part of its decision was based on the principle that, the law in its mercy, demands that a child should be subject to such correction as may tend to remove the causes, which have led the child to commit, acts inimical to society; where it might demand that an adult committing the same acts should be visited with a heavier punishment of deterrent effect. While the law does not say that a criminal under the age of sixteen is not subject to punishment for a crime, it says that proof of acts which would establish guilt of crime if committed by an adult does not establish the guilt of a child under the age of sixteen years, of any crime, but only of juvenile delinquency.

While a child under sixteen can be guilty of murder in the first or second degree where he kills a man with felonious intent, such felonious intent cannot be established without both proof and finding of intent to kill or of *guilt of an independent felony* during which the homicide occurred. Though, a person who with evil mind commits a crime may, in the interests of society, be punished even by death for the undesigned and unforeseen result of the crime, a child under the age of sixteen, should not be subject to death or life imprisonment as a result of the calamitous though undersigned acts, which are not criminal in their inception.

Note: Student must find the entire case for a complete case history and court opinion.

NOTES AND QUESTIONS

[1] Assume that in a juvenile proceeding, it was concluded that the child in question was indeed delinquent. Should that be the equivalent or ground for finding that the child did not commit the crime?

Notes:

[2] Do you consider it sound legal argument to conclude that because a child is able to appreciate the wrongfulness of his acts, should be enough ground to find him capable and responsible for the crime? Explain.

Notes:

[3] Consider the findings that children age 11 to 13 and a fifth of those 14 or 15 understand legal matters at a similar level as mentally ill adults found incompetent to stand trial. Based on such findings, should a child age 14 found and proven to have the IQ of an adult be declared incompetent to stand trial? Think about the argument that the issue should be what the law says the physical *age* of capacity is and not about the mental age of the child. Do you agree with such argument? Why and why not?

Notes:

[4] 'In answer to the increase in the number of juvenile crime and a lack of trust in the rehabilitation efforts, about 47 states since 1992 have adopted laws lowering the age at which juveniles may stand trial as adults.' (See Wayne R. LaFave, *Modern Criminal Law supra; note 4 P. 485,* In ref. *41 Ariz.L.Rev. 193, 194 n.8 (1999)*)

Notes:

[5] "Like its adult counterpart, the juvenile justice system operates as a screening device. It shares with and complements the adult system's functions of imposing social controls and attributing blame. Moreover, as a consequence of juvenile proceedings, convicted youth may suffer the social stigma and loss of liberty associated with the adult criminal process. It follows that the commitment to punishing only the culpable that animates adult criminal jurisprudence should also be applicable to the juvenile process."[54] Do you agree with this notion? If so, do you think such application of justice serve the same purpose adult criminal process is designed serve?

---

[54] Andrew Walkover, *The Infancy Defense in the New Juvenile Court, 31 U.C.L.A. Rev. 503, 538 (1984)*

Notes:

[6] George was convicted in the criminal court of murder, armed robbery and electronic equipment theft. The said crimes were committed while George was 16, on appeal, he claimed the court erred in excluding evidence he was incapable of the crime based on his age at the time of commission. He maintained that his emotional maturity and his mental capacity would have shown he had a mental age of a ten- year-old and that the said conviction was in violation of the state law, which states that 'a person shall not be guilty of a crime unless he is age 13 years at the time of commission.' Based on such evidence, should George be found not guilty of the crimes on the ground of incapacity, based on his age? Do you think that due to judicial interpretation, it is fair to conclude the age referred to in the code is the mental age and not the biological age? Is it the legislative intent to include the mental age as claimed by George?

Notes: Please explain your answers to question (6) below. Look for a statute that provide defense for juvenile criminals and discuss the legislative motive for having such statutes as a shield for minors.

INSANITY DEFENSE

Another issue in criminal law is whether one legally considered of unsound mind or disturbed faculty, be made to answer for a crime or act he has committed. Should one found to be of mental disease, or a mind so disturbed that he cannot understand the charges against him be made to stand trial until his disease and troubled mind is restored? These and many issues are considered in criminal proceedings in order to prevent a miscarriage of justice.

At various points in a criminal case, the issue of insanity is considered relevant and important. The first issue is to determine whether at the time of the alleged crime the defendant is of sound mind and mental capacity to appreciate his act. If his mental ability is of such character and degree as to negative criminal responsibility, such a determination will entitle him to an acquittal. The second issue to be raised is at the time set for arraignment. If the mind of one indicted is so disturbed by mental infirmities that he is unable to understand the charge against him and to plead intelligently thereto, he should not be permitted to plead until his faculty is restored. The third issue deals with the mental state of the defendant at the time of trial. Mental disorder at such stage has nothing to do with the issue of guilt or innocence, unless it may have some tendency to show the mental state of the defendant at the time of commission of said act. "But one whose mental condition is now so disturbed that he is unable to understand the charge against him, and possible defenses thereto, and hence is unable properly to advise with his counsel in regard to the conduct of the trial, ought not to be tried now, whatever his mental condition may have been at the time of the alleged crime. Hence upon such a finding the defendant is committed to some proper hospital. He is to remain there until his reason is restored, at which time he is to be returned to the court for trial. If he is to be committed beyond a reasonable time, it is necessary to resort to regular commitment procedure."[55]

The next and fourth issue is raised at the time of allocution, when the defendant is asked after a verdict or pleads of guilty if he knows of any reason why judgment should not be rendered against him. A finding of insanity at such stage will trigger the defendant's confinement to a mental institution until his reason returns; for in the words of Blackstone: 'If, after he be tried

[55] Jackson v. Indiana, 406 U.S. 715, 92 S.Ct. 1845 (1972)

See also Jones v. United States, U.S. 103 S.Ct. 3043 (1983) Where a defendant is acquitted on the grounds of insanity he may be committed pending a determination that he has regained his sanity and may be kept beyond the period for which defendant may have been kept had the defendant been convicted. The defendant's insanity must be established by a preponderance of evidence and due process standards must be satisfied in determining the need for commitment.

and found guilty, he loses his senses before judgment, judgment shall not be pronounced. ... For peradventure says the humanity of the English law, had the prisoner been of sound memory, he might have alleged something in stay of judgment. ..."[56]

The final and fifth issue is raised at the time of execution of judgment, for example, in capital cases. This is based on the principle that one must not be put to death while of unsound mind, for if he is of sound mind, he might be able to mount a defense in stay of his execution.[57]

Finally, it is important to mention that nature and extent of mental disorder, that will entitle the defendant to an acquittal, has become an issue in criminal law in dealing with insanity cases. The issue is not whether the defendant was once of sound faculty, which has deteriorated due to a disease or injury or as a result of mental deficiency at birth. However, the sole determinant and important is the nature and extent of defendant's mental abnormality. Also, while a mental disease may be so severe as to negate criminal culpability, there is no uniformity as to the type of disorder required for insanity cases.

---

[56] Rollin M. Perkins, *Criminal Law and Procedure; P.595* in ref. (*4 Bl.Comm. 24-25*)

[57] Solesbee v. Balkcom, *339 U.S. 9, 70 S.Ct. 457 (1950)* where one under sentence of death asked the governor to postpone execution on the ground that he had become insane after conviction. Under authority of a state statute the governor appointed three doctors who examined the convict and declared him sane. In denying relief in habeas corpus proceedings the court held that this procedure was not a denial of due process under the Fourteenth Amendment.

TESTS FOR INSANITY

M'NAGHTEN'S CASE

House of Lords, 1843
8 Eng.Rep. 718, 10 Cl. & Fin. 200

In the M'Naghten's case, the court was asked to determine the proper test for insanity, in a situation, where the defendant claims to be insane at the time the crime is committed. In this case, Daniel M'Naghten shot and killed Edward Drummond, a private secretary to Sir Robert Peel. At the time of the crime, M'Naghten believed that Peel was heading a conspiracy to kill him, he had intended to take Peel's life, but instead, he shot Drummond because he mistakenly believed him to be Peel. At the trial, M'Naghten claimed that he was insane and therefore, not responsible for the crime because it was his delusions, which caused him to act.

The jury agreed, and M'Naghten was found not guilty by reason of insanity. Due to the importance of Drummond and the intended victim, Sir Robert Peel, the decision was not a popular one. After series of debates in The House of Lords over the decision, The House asked the Justices of the Queen's Bench five questions concerning the standards for acquitting a defendant due to his insanity.

The most important answer by the Justices, deals with the fact that a defendant, will not have the defense of insanity, unless at the time of the alleged crime, he was laboring under such a defect of reason, from disease of the mind, such that he does not to know the nature and quality of what he was doing; or, if he did know it, that he did not know he was doing what was wrong. The answer is what has come to be known as the M'Naghten rule.

Note: To see the five questions posed by the House of Lords and the answers, please find and read the entire M'Naghten's case.

QUESTIONS

Refer to the response by the justices to the fourth question in the case; based on the answer given, if one under the influence of a delusion supposes another man to be in the act of attempting to take his life, and he kills that man, as he supposes in self-defense, he would not be liable in punishment.

However, if he kills based on a delusion that the deceased had inflicted a serious injury to his character and fortune, he would be liable to punishment. Explain why it is excusable to kill in self-defense while under a delusion but not excusable to do so in protection of property. In your own view, do you think the justices believed killing in self-defense is more legally reasonable than killing in protection of Character and fortune? In your opinion, what role does fact and reality play in the answer to the fourth question? Do you think the Justices have the use of *excessive force* in mind in their response to the fourth question? Please explain your answers in details; a Yes or No answer alone will not do for the questions.

NOTE: In State v. Boan, *235 Kan. 800, 686 P.2d 160 (1984)*, expert testimony revealed that Boan had a feeling of being God or his representative, who was present with him at the Last Supper, and that he believed some persons were in his body trying to displace him, making him to defend himself the way he did from "salvation level attacks." Based on testimony, defendant was aware of the laws of the state that it was wrong to shoot someone but due to his "religious delusion" he "modified the definition of what was right, according to his belief that he, as God made the rights." In affirming his murder conviction, the court upheld the following instruction: "Right and wrong are used here in their legal sense, not the social or moral sense. 'Wrong' means that which is prohibited by law."

Notes:

Devon a resident of Brooklyn New York, believed the NYPD hated him and was out to get him. Devon knew his belief was unreasonable because he had never been treated badly by the police. Still consumed by his belief, Devon armed himself with an AK-47, ambushed and killed a NY police officer.

Devon is charged with murder and he has mounted the defense of insanity. He is most likely to be found not guilty, if the jurisdiction subscribed to

  (A) The Felony Murder rule
  (B) The doctrine of self-defense
  (C) The Model Penal Code
  (D) The M'Naghten rule
  (E) The Castle Doctrine
  (F) None of the above

DAVIS V. STATE

Supreme Court of Tennessee (1930)
161 Tenn. 23, 28 S.W.2d 993

Based on facts, the plaintiff Davis was indicted for killing L.R. Noe and convicted of murder in the second degree. ... After deliberation, the Jury found that the defendant was insane on the issue of the relationship between his late wife and Noe, but they also found that he knew the difference between right and wrong, and as a result, they asked the court what to do under such situation.

In answer, the court read to the jury a part of his charge previously given them and added other instructions. The court rejected the argument that, due to mental disease, the will power of the defendant was so impaired that, he was unable to resist the impulse to kill Noe, therefore, should not be guilty, although, he could determine between right and wrong as to the particular act.

The Prosecution argued that, though, plaintiff acted under an irresistible impulse produced by an insane delusion he would still be guilty if he could distinguish between right and wrong and knew that it was wrong to kill Noe.

The defense counter that, there may be a mental disease destroying the faculty of volition, of choosing, as well as mental disease destroying the faculty of perception, and that any of both conditions would relief defendant of criminal accountability.

The court refused to recognize as a defense destroyed volition, even as a result of mental disease, apart from destroyed perception.

In its final ruling, the Supreme Court rejected the conviction of murder in the second degree and remanded the case, due to lack of proof. The court stated that, It is not necessary that a defendant's reason be dethroned to mitigate a killing to manslaughter and therefore, it is error so to instruct a jury. According to the opinion, if the excitement and passion adequately aroused obscures, the reason of the defendant, the killing will be reduced to manslaughter. A defendant acting under such temporary mental stress is presumed to lack malice, an essential element of murder. Malice cannot be imputed to a defendant when his reason is not merely obscured but has been swept away and kept away by an insane delusion under which he acts. Such a defendant cannot be guilty of murder.

Note: Please research Davis v. State, to read the entire case background and court deliberations.

NOTES

[1] The fact that a defendant is successful with his insanity defense does not mean he goes free without consequences for his crime. In some cases, a successful insanity defense may end up as an empty undertaking, since the disposition of consequences for a successful insanity defense, does not look better than that imposed via a conviction. In most cases, a successful insanity defense will lead to the confinement of the defendant to a mental institution for the rest of his life and without the possibility of ever getting out.

[2] A defendant confined to a mental institution in most cases, may assume the label as a 'maniac' unfit to live among normal people due to the danger such integration and association with people may pose.

[3] The prospect of release from a mental institution is slim even after the mental abnormality is corrected or the defendant is believed to have regained his reasons. He is still consider a danger to the society and as such, must remain in a mental hospital.

[4] In some cases, the court is allowed to enter a not guilty plea based on insanity on behalf of a defendant when it is found necessary. However, to enter such a plea *sua sponte*, the court must weigh many factors including the defense opposition to an insanity defense, the court personal observation of the defendant, and the reasonableness of the defendant's decision. The court must also consider the viability of the defense and the likely nature of the consequences should an insanity defense be pursued.[58]

[5] The rationale for considering such factors as mentioned above in the pursuit of justice, is expressed in United States v. Wright, *627 F.2d 1300 (D.C. Circuit 1980)* where it was said that, the "society has an obligation, through the insanity defense, to withhold punishment of someone not blameworthy." *Wright* was later overruled in United States v. Marble, *940 F.2d 1543 (D.C.Cir.1991)*.

---

[58] State v. Jones, *99 Wash.2d 735, 664 P.2d 1216 (1983)* where it was held that the Trial Court committed prejudicial error by entering a not guilty by reason of insanity plea over defendant's objection.

[6] A competent defendant has the right to refuse an NGI, (Not Guilty by Insanity) as long as he is competent to make such a plea and does make an intelligent and voluntary waiver. An issue is whether such a defendant, be allowed to refuse an NGI even at the refusal of his counsel?[59]

DIMINISHED CAPACITY

Diminished capacity is a Common Law doctrine that allows proof of defendant's mental condition, on the issue of his capacity to form the specific intent in situations where specific intent, must be proved as an element of the crime charged. In *State v. Gramenz, 256 Iowa 134, 126 N.W.2d 285* (1964), the court held that evidence of a defendant's mental unsoundness might be received to negate specific intent for the crime charged, premeditation and deliberation on a charge of first degree murder. The court refused to allow the evidence on the elements of malice aforethought and general criminal intent. According to the court: 'While malice aforethought is the specific state of mind necessary to convict of murder, it is far different from the specific intent which is a necessary element of murder in the first degree; it may be express or implied from the acts and conduct of defendant.'[60]

Some jurisdiction have gone as far as to limit the effect of the evidence of mental disease or defect relating to criminal culpability generally, as it would undercut legislative intent to extend the defense of diminished capacity to cases where the defense is not applicable. For example, Iowa common law recognized mental impairment other than legal insanity as a defense only to specific intent crimes at the time the state insanity defense was codified. 'The legislature thus established the applicable legal standard for deciding culpability upon evidence of mental impairment in cases requiring proof only of guilty knowledge or general criminal intent accompanying a prohibited act. The mens rea of those crimes is not affected by evidence of mental impairment that does not meet the insanity standard.'[61]

In most U.S. jurisdictions that recognize the defense of diminished capacity, the defense is only available to specific intent crimes and according to the **Insanity Defense Act of 1984,** *18 U.S.C. §*

[59] State v. Lowenfield, *495 So.2d 1245 (La.1985)*: "It appears beyond argument that when a competent defendant wishes to plead not guilty rather than not guilty by reason of insanity, and clearly understands the consequences of his choice, then the counsel must acquiesce to the wishes of his competent client. The court had no choice but to allow the defendant to withdraw his pleas and in this we find no error." See also United States v Laura, 607 F.2d 52 (3d Cir. 1979) where it was reiterated, "a defendant has the right to decide, within limits, the type of defense he wishes to mount."

[60] See Wayne R. LaFave et al, *Modern Criminal Law supra*; P. 434 ref. *State v. Gramenz, supra,*

[61] Wayne R. LaFave, Modern *Criminal Law supra; P.435 ref. State v. McVey, 376 N.W.2d 585 (1985)*

17: It is an affirmative defense to a prosecution under any Federal Statute that, during commission of the act leading to the offense, the defendant, due to a severe mental disease or defect, could not appreciate the nature and quality or the wrongfulness of his acts. Mental disease or defect does not otherwise constitute a defense.

This opinion was debated in *United States v. Pohlot, 827 F.2d 889* (3rd Cir. 1987), where the government claimed that such a language prevents a defendant from using evidence of mental abnormality to negate mens rea. The court disagreed, reiterating that "Both the wording of the statute and the legislative history, leave no doubt that Congress intended, as the Senate report stated, to bar only alternative 'affirmative defenses' that 'excuse' misconduct and evidence that disproves an element of the crime itself".

According to *Pohlot*, 'mental disease or defect is admissible whenever it is relevant to prove that the defendant did or did not have a state of mind that is an element of the offense; *Model Penal Code § 4.02(1) (1962)*. Although this principle has sometimes been phrased as a version of the 'diminished capacity defense,' it does not provide any grounds for acquittal not provided in the definition of the offense'. Properly understood, it is therefore not a defense at all but merely a rule of evidence.'[62]

American jurisdictions adopt one of four views in deciding whether to take or reject diminished capacity evidence. Each jurisdiction follows either the mens rea model, the partial responsibility model, or it may reject the admission of such evidence as a defense in the case. The four views recognized in the United States are: (1) the admission of any evidence of a mental abnormality only to negate the state of mind required as an element of the offense charged, (2) the admission of mental abnormality as evidence only in homicide cases, to negate malice aforethought or premeditation required as an element of homicide, (3) the admission of evidence of mental abnormality to negate the specific intent required as an element of the offense charged or (4) to reject the admission of mental abnormality, as evidence unless the defendant shows a mental state that rises to the level of insanity.

In essence, not all American jurisdictions allow the defendant to use diminished capacity as evidence and those that allow it are specific as to how and when it may be used.

---

[62] Wayne R. LaFave, supra P.437; ref United *States v. Pohlot*, supra

ALCOHOLISM AND INTOXICATION

Another issue in criminal law is whether one intoxicated and controlled by the presence of alcohol in his system, should be deemed to possess the required intent to commit the crime charged. Prior to the nineteenth century, drunkenness was not considered a defense in criminal prosecution. However, in the present day, there are some changes to the strict rule. For example, involuntary or innocent intoxication may be so severe that the defendant can be found not guilty of the crime charged; even though, he committed the crime. He is without fault due to the role alcohol played in the crime if indeed his intoxication is found to be innocent. On the other hand, one found to be voluntarily intoxicated can also be exculpated if the crime charged is one that requires a specific intent, a state of mind necessary to find one guilty of such crime. If at the time of commission the defendant was highly intoxicated such that he lacked the required state of mind to commit such a crime, he may not be liable for the offense. Also, one who suffers from delirium is treated the same as other forms of insanity although, it may have been due to overuse of alcohol.

As earlier indicated, if the crime charged requires a specific intent, the one charged is not guilty if at the time of commission, he was too overcome by alcohol and completely intoxicated to form the state of mind necessary for the crime. In addition, it must be established that the defendant, did not entertain the intent to commit the crime prior to his intoxication. Suppose **D** has been indicted for burglary, the charges show that **D** broke into the house of **X** at night with the intent to steal. The evidence shows that **D** opened the front door of **X's** house late at night, went in and was found in a drunken stupor on the floor. **D** was searched and as it turned out, he had taken nothing. **D** was tried and the jury is satisfied that while he managed to stumble into **X's** house before he lost consciousness, his mind was too befogged with drinks to be capable of entertaining any intent. Such a finding will not support a conviction of burglary.[63] The defendant in this case may not be guilty of burglary because the specific intent required to commit such a felony is missing therefore, he is excusable.

***Note: Read* BURROWS v. STATE**, Supreme Court of Arizona, *38 Ariz. 99, 297 P. 1029 (1931)*

---

[63] Rollin M. Perkins et al, *Criminal Law and Procedure supra; P.625 ref. State v. Philips, 80 W.Va. 748, 93 S.W. 828 (1917).* And a fumbling effort to get into a building by one too drunk to be capable of entertaining any intent is not an attempt to commit burglary. *People v. Jones, 263 Ill.564, 105 N.E. 744 (1914)*

NOTES

[1] Intoxication resulting from a physician's prescription is involuntary, even if an overdose was inadvertently taken. *State v. Gilchrist, 15 Wash.App. 892, 552 P.2d 690 (1976)*

[2] One could not properly be convicted of driving while under the influence of drugs, if the drug he was using had been given him by his doctor with no warning that its use while driving was prohibited, *Crutchfield v. State, 627 P.2d 196 (Alaska 1981)*

[3] One who strikes a woman with a car, and did not stop to give aid, is guilty of not stopping and giving aid even if he did not know he had hit her, if the only reason he did not know was because he was drunk. *Martinez v. State, 137 Tex. Cr.R. 434, 128 S.W.2d 398 (1939)*[64]

[4] There are cases where the defendant may try to use voluntary intoxication as a defense to negate the mental state required for the crime charged. ***Montana v. Egelhoff, 516 U.S. 37, 116 S.Ct. 2013, 135 L.Ed.2d 361 (1996)***: In July 1992 the defendant while camping in the Yaak region of northwestern Montana to pick mushroom, met Roberta Pavola and John Christenson, who were also picking mushroom. On Sunday, July 12, they all sold the mushroom they had collected and spent the rest of the day and evening drinking in bars and at a private party in Troy, Montana. At about 9 p.m., they left the party in a 1974 Ford Galaxy station wagon belonging to Christenson and continued their drinking binge.

At around midnight, officers of the Lincoln County, sheriff department, discovered the station wagon stuck in a ditch along U.S. Highway 2. The bodies of Pavola and Christenson were found in the front seat, each dead from a gunshot to the head. Defendant was found alive in the rear of the car yelling obscenities. His blood-alcohol level was 36 percent over one hour after the incident. Defendant's 38-caliber handgun was also found on the floor of the car, near the brake pedal, with four loaded rounds and two empty casings; gunshot residue was found on defendant's hands.

Defendant provided evidence that he was intoxicated; however, the jury was instructed it could not consider defendant's intoxicated condition. In determining the existence of a mental state required for the offense, the jury found defendant guilty of both counts and the court sentenced him to 84 years imprisonment. On appeal, the Supreme Court of Montana reversed the court's

---

[64] Note: This may not apply to one whose unconsciousness was due to voluntary intoxication. *People v. Anderson, 87 Cal.App.2d 857, 197 P.2d 839 (1948)*

decision. The court's decision to reverse was based on the principle that the Due Process Clause guarantees a defendant the right to present and have considered by the jury *"all relevant evidence"* to counter the state's evidence on all elements of the offense charged.

[5] In *State v. Castillo,* the defendant Castillo, who had been drinking and had engaged in an argument with Rios, left the bar and returned an hour and a half later. He pointed a gun at Rios who was 14 feet away, said, "I kill you", and fired one shot, which was fatal. Having been convicted of murder in the first degree, he appealed. Defendant claimed that the trial court erroneously instructed the jury on the issue of voluntary manslaughter in that, it failed to inform the jury that defendant could be convicted of manslaughter if he had intentionally committed the killing, yet because of diminished capacity, did not act with malice.[65]

In reversing the trial court's judgment, the appeals court, stated that the error claimed by the defendant lies not in the language of the instructions but in their inadequacy. Although, the trial court correctly instructed the jury that it must not convict defendant of *murder* without proof of malice, it failed to instruct the jury that it could convict defendant of *voluntary manslaughter* if it found that defendant had intentionally taken life but in so doing, lacked malice because of diminished capacity due to mental defect, mental illness, or intoxication. The court decided to reverse the conviction, on the grounds that the trial court failed to give the instruction set out in *People v. Conley, supra 64 Cal.2d 310. ...*

[6] In *State v. Mash, 323 N.C. 339, 372 S.E.2d 532* (1988), the defendant was charged with first degree murder and the jury was instructed that "the intoxication must be so great that his mind and reason were so completely overthrown so as to render him utterly incapable to form a deliberate and premeditated purpose to kill. Mere intoxication cannot serve as an excuse for the defendant. It must be intoxication to the extent that defendant's mental processes were so overcome by the excessive use of liquor or other intoxicants that he had temporarily, at least, lost the capacity to think and plan." The court declared the instructions erroneous since they "impose on the jury the standard applicable to defendant's burden of production at trial, a burden defendant must meet before being entitled to voluntary intoxication instructions at all..." According to the court, though, meeting such a standard is a "prerequisite" to defendant's getting a voluntary intoxication instructions, the standard may not be applied to the jury's consideration of "intoxication evidence." The jury must decide based on intoxication evidence and all other evidence in the case, whether reasonable doubt exists defendant formed a "deliberate

---

[65] *People v. Conley, 64 Cal.2d 310, 318, 49 Cal.Rptr. 815, 411 P.2d 911 (1966)*

and premeditated" intent to kill, not whether his intoxication was so great making him incapable of forming such an intent. That is, "to find for defendant on the intoxication issue, the jury does not have to conclude that his intoxication rendered defendant 'utterly incapable' of forming the necessary intent; it need only conclude that because of his intoxication either defendant did not form the requisite intent or there is at least a reasonable doubt about it."[66]

[7] Voluntary intoxication is a defense only if it negatives some required element of the crime in question. It is not enough that it puts the defendant in a state of mind that resembles insanity. Involuntary intoxication on the other hand, does constitute a defense if it puts the defendant in such a state of mind such that, he does not know the nature and quality of his act or know that his act is wrong, in a jurisdiction which has incorporated the M'Naghten test for insanity.

[8] One of the requirements for the reduction of an *intentional* homicide from murder down to voluntary manslaughter is that the defendant must have been provoked into a reasonable loss of self-control by his victim's conduct. However, defendant's *voluntary* intoxication, which unreasonably provokes him, will not satisfy to reduce his homicide to manslaughter. Note: *Montana is one of the states where by statute; voluntary intoxication may not be taken into consideration, in determining the presence of a mental state.*

[9] The majority view is that though, intoxication can negative a required *intention* it is not enough to negative recklessness. It is the principle of the law that intoxication having reduced the crime from first degree to second degree murder, it cannot further reduce the homicide from second degree murder to manslaughter; the reason for such view is that in most jurisdictions with degrees of murder, one may be guilty of second degree murder by killing without any intent to kill or cause bodily harm but with a high degree of *recklessness*.

[10] **MPC 208 (4)** makes intoxication a defense if it is not *self-induced*. **MPC 208 (5):** The definition of self-induced intoxication excludes the case of one brought to drunkenness by such *duress* as would afford a defense to a charge of crime.

[11] **MPC 208 (3):** Intoxication itself does not constitute mental disease; **MPC 208 (4):** intoxication which (a) is not self induced (b) is pathological is an affirmative defense if by reason of such intoxication the actor at the time of his conduct, lacks substantial capacity either to appreciate its criminality or to conform his conduct to the requirement of law.

---

[66] Wayne R. LaFave, *Modern Criminal Law supra; ref. State v. Mash, supra P. 473*

[12] **MPC 208 (2):** When recklessness establishes an element of the offense, if the actor due to self induced intoxication is unaware of a risk of which he would have been aware had he been sober, such unawareness is immaterial.

NOTE: *The majority view is that involuntary intoxication is a defense only when it is accompanied by temporary insanity; however, it has commonly been held that voluntary intoxication is not a defense, where the offense is one requiring a general intent.* Intoxication can be of four kinds: coerced intoxication, pathological intoxication, unexpected intoxication (such as in the use of a prescribed medication) and intoxication by innocent mistake.

ACTION OF THE VICTIM

In *Embry v. Commonwealth, 236 Ky. 204, 32 S.W.2d 979* (1930), a man threw a blasting powder into an open fireplace. An explosion occurred, setting fire to the building, causing the wife and the 19 year-old son of the host to burn to death. Several people some of them younger were able to get out of the house safely while some so unfortunate were killed. The court found the defendant not entitled to an instruction that he be excused, if those who did not reach safety had failed to use due care in the effort. In another situation, the defendants ran over and killed a pedestrian while driving a horse and a carriage at higher rate than normal while intoxicated. Defendants want excused because deceased, who was deaf, was fond of walking in the middle of the road at various time of the day and night. The court disagrees that defendants be excused.[67]

While contributory negligence may not be a defense for an action otherwise criminal in nature, the law sometimes, looks to the conduct of the victim rather than ignore it, to determine if his actions have a bearing on whether or not the defendant was culpable.

---

[67] *Regina v. Longbottom and Another, 3 Cox C.C. 439 (1849).* Also, *Regina v. Kew, 12 Cox C.C. 355 (1872)*

HUBBARD V. COMMONWEALTH

Court of Appeals of Kentucky
304 Ky. 818, 202 S.W.2d 634 (1947)

According to evidence, R.W. Dyche died of a heart attack. Robert Hubbard was found guilty of killing him and sentenced to two years' imprisonment on a voluntary manslaughter charge. The trial took place in Jackson County on a change of venue.

Based on facts presented, Hubbard was at home on Furlough from the army in August 1945. He was arrested for being drunk in a public place and presented before the Judge of Laurel County. As a result of his state of intoxication, he was ordered to jail, but refused to go peaceably. Dyche, the jailer, and Newman, a deputy, took hold of him. The prisoner resisted and struck Newman. In the struggle both fell to the floor and Hubbard lay on his back "kicking at" anybody or anything within reach. Dyche had hold of him. He said, "I have done all I can; you will have to help me," or "somebody is going to have to take my place; I am done." Judge Boggs took hold of the criminal and persuaded him to get up; but he continued to resist as he was being taken to jail by Newman and another person. Dyche followed them out of the courthouse. He put his hand over his heart and sat down. In a few minutes he got down on the ground where he "rolled and tumbled" until he died within a half hour. Hubbard never struck Dyche and evidence revealed Dyche had suffered for some time with a serious heart condition, and had remarked to a friend several hours before that he was feeling bad. Three doctors testified that his death was due to acute dilation of the heart, but that the physical exercise and excitement was calculated to accelerate his death.

The Court of appeal was called to determine whether the facts constitute involuntary manslaughter. In its decision to reverse the conviction, the court indicated that the misdemeanor of the defendant was too remote-not in time, to be the cause of death. It further stated that, the failure of the man's diseased heart caused his demise.[68] That the intervening act of the diseased in rolling and tumbling in pain on the courthouse yard, instead of lying quiet and still, was probably as much responsible for his ensuing death coupled with the initial excitement caused by the accused's conduct.

Note: Research the case Hubbard v. Commonwealth, for the entire case and complete court opinion.

---

[68] Livingston v. Commonwealth, *14 Grat. Va., 592*

In **Regina v. Holland,** *2 Moody & R. 351, 174 Eng.Rep. 313,* the defendant a prisoner, was involved in a fight and charged with inflicting several mortal blows and wound upon Thomas Garland, which caused a cut upon one of his fingers.

Based on evidence the victim had been waylaid and assaulted by the prisoner and he also sustained a severe cut across one of his fingers by an iron instrument. The surgeon urged him to have the finger amputated, telling him unless it was amputated, his life would be in great danger. Victim refused to have his finger amputated and day-to-day; he came to the surgeon to have his wound dressed. After a while, lockjaw, induced by the cut, attacked the wound causing the finger to be amputated, but at the time it was too late to save the victim who died from the infection. The surgeon indicated that had the finger been amputated when he so advised, he thought it most probable the life of the victim would have been saved.

The prisoner claimed the cause of death was not the wound caused on the deceased, but rather, the refusal of the deceased to submit to proper surgical treatment, that could have prevented his death.

In finding defendant guilty, the judge was of the opinion the defendant's claim was no defense and informed the jury that if defendant willfully, and without any justifiable cause, caused the wound upon the deceased, and the wound is concluded to be the cause of death, the defendant was guilty of murder; for it serves no purpose and made no difference whether the wound was by itself mortal, or it became the cause of death by deceased's negligence to obtain better treatment as advised by the surgeon. The issue is, whether in the end the wound inflicted by defendant was the cause of death.

Chapter Ten
Special Defenses

Public Authority

There are certain acts, which if done by order of a superior or under the protection of public authority, are not considered crimes. If a police officer shoots and kills one holding a knife to his wife's throat and about to slaughter her, the police office may not be guilty of any crime if he acted reasonably and under public authority. Likewise, a soldier who killed an enemy combatant is not guilty of any crime; the killing is considered an act of war done under the protection of public authority and within the rules of war. Also, one who carried out the execution of a defendant found guilty and sentenced to death, is not guilty of such killing, the execution is a court order and therefore, the executioner has acted under the protection of public authority.

While public authority if reasonably used can make a defendant not guilty of the crime charged, unreasonable use of it will completely remove the privilege, such that one found to have abused its protection might be reasonably charged and convicted. For example, a police officer, that shot and killed an unarmed offender who signified his willingness to surrender by raising his arms, may have abused his authority and be properly charged for the killing. Even in the time of war, an enemy may not be killed needlessly after he has been disarmed and securely imprisoned.[69]

Only the one privileged to use such authority or his duly appointed deputy might carry out the sentence of death.[70] Also, in exercising such authority, the privileged officer, may not substitute one method of execution for another. For example, if the court order and sentence is that the convicted offender be executed by hanging, the executioner may not turn around and choose another method of execution such as, death via the electric chair. An executioner, who defies

---

[69] "That it is legal to kill an alien enemy in the heat and exercise of war is undeniable; but to kill such an enemy after he has laid down his arms, and especially when he is confined in prison, is murder." *State v. Gut, 13 Minn. (Gil. Ed.) 315, 330 (1868)*

[70] (See 4 Bl. Comm. 179)

order of the court by electing another method of killing, abused his authority and privilege and therefore, would be guilty of a homicide.

A willful abuse of authority will also destroy the privilege, making the excessive flogging of a disobedient convict, by a guard, to constitute criminal assault and battery.[71]

---

[71] State v. Mincher, *172 N.C. 895, 90 S.E. 429 (1916)*

COMMONWEALTH EX REL. WADSWORTH V. SHORTALL

Supreme Court of Pennsylvania
206 Pa. 165, 55 A. 952 (1903)

Wadsworth was a private in a division of the National Guard that had been ordered out by the governor to suppress disorder and violence beyond the control of local authorities. He was posted to guard a house at night and told to halt all prowlers or persons approaching the house. His order was to "shoot to kill" anyone who refused to stop when asked to do so. At about 11:30 o'clock a stranger approached the house. Wadsworth called "halt" four times. The command was ignored by the stranger, he opened the gate and continued into the yard, after which he was shot and killed by Wadsworth. Wadsworth was arrested and charged with manslaughter. To inquire into the legality of his imprisonment the presiding justice of this court allowed a writ of habeas corpus.

In its final judgment, the Supreme Court found Wadsworth, not guilty. The decision was based partly on the principle that, unless in a case of excessive use of authority, or where the order by a superior is illegal, where at first blush it is apparent and palpable to the commonest understanding that the order is illegal, the law will excuse a military subordinate, when acting in obedience to the order of his commander. The court referenced *Riggs v. State, 4 Cold. 85*, where the Supreme Court of Tennessee held that, "any order given by an officer to his private which does not expressly and clearly show on its face, or in the body thereof, its own illegality, the soldier would be bound to obey, and such order would be a protection to him."

The court declared Wadsworth not guilty of any crime, under the warrant held by respondent.[72]

---

[72] If a military detail is sent to kill an officer unlawfully the order given would not excuse the killing. But a member of the detail who did not know the mission and did not participate in the killing would not be guilty of the homicide. The rule that all conspirators are guilty by reason of the act of one in carrying out their unlawful agreement has no application to a soldier obeying orders with no knowledge of an intended unlawful purpose. *Riggs v. State, 43 Tenn. 85 (1866)* Also the acts of a subordinate done in compliance with an unlawful order given him by his superior are excused and impose no criminal liability upon him unless the superior's orders is one which a man of ordinary sense and understanding would, under the circumstances, know to be unlawful, or if the order in question is actually known to the accused to be unlawful." *State v. Calley, 483 F.2d 1401 (4ᵗʰ Cir. 1973)*

CRIME PREVENTION

40 C.J.S., Homicide, § 101 states the rule: "The taking of human life is justifiable when done for the prevention of any atrocious crime attempted to be committed with force…. A homicide is justifiable when committed by necessity and in good faith in order to prevent a felony attempted by force or surprise, such as murder, robbery, burglary, arson, rape, sodomy and the like… killing to prevent a felony is not justifiable if the felony is a *secret one, or unaccompanied by force, or if it does not involve the security of the person or home…*"Also 26 Am.jur., homicide *§172*, states the rule: "In general, it may be said that the law countenances the taking of human life in connection with the defense of property only *where an element of danger to the person of the slayer is present. …*" "The mere fact that such (personal) property is being wrongfully taken… does not justify a homicide committed in an attempt to prevent the taking or detention."

The law gives the privilege to act in prevention of a crime and in defense of person or property. The aforementioned privileges are available to one under the authority to use them. The beneficiary may use reasonable force to achieve both necessities however, "it is not necessary that he should intervene solely for the purpose of protecting the public order or of protecting the private interests imperiled. His act, though a single one, may well be done for both purposes. If so, either privilege is available to him."[73]

At this junction it is essential to reiterate that anyone is privileged to intervene for the purpose of preventing the commission of a crime or its consummation therefore. Nonetheless, a person using such privilege must do so with care and act reasonably such that the use of force is not excessive or resort to measures, which under the circumstances of the case may be deemed unnecessary. Also, the use of such privilege to prevent the commission of a minor misdemeanor, has limited support since in the absence of legislative authority, the privilege to intervene for the purpose of preventing the commission or consummation of a crime does not authorize the use of force in the case of a misdemeanor, which is not a breach of the peace.

In essence, the use of deadly force to prevent a crime has limited scope. Such use of force is only encouraged, in situations likely to cause death or serious bodily harm and acts within the general scope of the preventive privilege. However, if one uses deadly force though, not intended but likely to cause death or serious bodily harm, his action will amount to a battery; if indeed, evidence show the force was in excess of that believed to be reasonable in the case.

---

[73] Restatement, Second, Torts, Scope Note to c. 5, Topic 2 (1965)

VILIBORGHI V. STATE

Supreme Court of Arizona
45 Ariz. 275, 43 P.2d 210 (1935)

Tried for murder, defendant was convicted of manslaughter. He conducted a store in the front of the building in which he lived. Based on defendant's testimony, the store had been burglarized on several occasions, during one of which a shot had been fired at him. On the night in question he was awakened by noises in the front of the building and went to investigate, taking a revolver with him, thinking that burglars were attempting to break into the building. Seeing a human hand reaching through the front window, and believing that his life and property were in danger, he fired through the window and immediately heard footfalls of persons running away. After the noise ceased he investigated and found the body of deceased laying on the sidewalk and beside it a jar of preserves and a bottle of pickles which had evidently been taken from a shelf adjacent to the broken window through which he saw the hand entering. The defense was based on a claim of justification, and an appeal was taken on the ground (among several others) that error was committed in the instructions to the jury.

The Supreme Court rejected the instructions, reversed the case and remanded for a new trial. The decision to reverse was based on the opinion that the defendant did not have a fair and impartial trial guarantee by the law. The court also cited the principle of the law that, the owner of the premises burglarized may, at any stage of the burglary, kill the burglar if it be reasonably necessary to prevent the final completion of his felonious purpose, regardless at what stage of the crime the shooting occurs. Even after completion of the burglary and the burglar is withdrawing from the scene of his crime, he may use all reasonably necessary force available, for the apprehension of a fleeing offender.

Note: *The student must research the case Viliborghi v. State, to read the entire case background and court opinion.*

SELF DEFENSE

No doubt we all have the reflexes of self-defense at the moment of birth. It is innate and we react in self-defense whenever we feel the impulses or it is necessary to do so. If a fly lands on your shoulder, you are quick to react by swapping it off either with the palm of your hand or a paper towel. It is foreign to your body, you dislike it being on you and therefore, you do not want to catch a disease from such a creature. Likewise, when you walk in the street and someone accidentally steps on your foot, you are quick to react depending on the magnitude of the force exerted; you are either push the person away if the foot has prior injury and you feel pain, or you just tell her to excuse you if there is no injury to the area stepped on.

It is fair to say that the ability to act in self-defense has been in place before it became a legal phenomenon and a recognized defense in criminal law. Each individual reacts differently in self-defense; the force used can either be reasonable or unreasonable. Take for example in the analogy above, it would be ironic for one with a fly on his shoulder to stab the fly with a knife while on his shoulder, or to take a gun and shoot the fly in an attempt to drive it away. To do so, would be both unnecessary and unreasonable force; his act will not only put his life in danger but that of others around him as well. Likewise, one who had his foot stepped on accidentally would be acting unreasonably and with excessive force, if he decides to strike the other party with a hammer (a deadly object) just for stepping on him, or by striking her with the butt of a gun to the face in self-defense. Irrespective of his innocence, use of such unreasonable force, would make the actor liable in battery including both civil and other criminal sanctions.

The use of reasonable or unreasonable force is dependent upon the nature of the force itself and the circumstances that triggered its use. Nonetheless the fact that the force exerted is deadly or not, a deadly or non-deadly force can be either reasonable or unreasonable depending on the situation of each case. Deadly force is unreasonable if non-deadly force is obviously sufficient to prevent the threatened harm. (Etter v. State, *185 Tenn. 218, 205 S.W.2d 1[1947]*); for example, one who is slapped slightly on the back, does not need to strike the aggressor with a hammer or a baseball bat, a more reasonable force of the same magnitude and that is not deadly will do to deter the threatened harm.

On the other hand, non-deadly force is unreasonable if it is obviously and substantially in excess of what is needed for the particular defense. (People v. Moody, *62 Cal.App.2d 18, 143 P.2d 978 [1943]*; for example, if one comes to your home uninvited and evidence shows he has not come to create harm, it would be unwise to kick the person in order to turn him away, a warning and a word of mouth such as "get out," alone will do in such a situation. Or if during a fracas the other party decides to pour cold water on you, you may reciprocate by pouring cold water on him in return, or use a more reasonable and non-deadly force. But if instead of cold water, you chose to pour hot water on his person, such action will amount to the use of both deadly and unreasonable force. While you may act by using the same magnitude of force exerted that is (cold water), the use of hot water is excessive force and normally, "use of excessive force constitutes battery." (Coleman v. State, *320 A.2d 740 [Del. 1974]*)

The privilege of an actor to use force in an attempt to prevent harm threatened (actually or apparently) by the wrongful act of another, should be based upon the reasonable belief of the defender under the circumstances of the case. One who has knocked down another while acting under the reasonable belief that his action was necessary in order to avoid being stabbed, is not guilty of battery even though, evidence later show that the other party had no intention to harm but was just playing a joke with a rubber dagger; (*Restatement, Second, Torts § 63, Illustrations 5, 9 (1965)*).

Depending on the situation, some states follow what is known as the "retreat rule" and others the "no retreat rule" however, this is not absolute since no jurisdiction requires or permit a "standing of your ground" in all situations; there are three approaches: If you are without fault and a victim of assault and a murderous attack, you are entitled to stand your ground and defend yourself, with deadly force if this reasonably seems necessary for your protection.

On the other hand, if you are the aggressor that is, responsible for the events that ensued say for example, in a fist fight and you realize the other party has resulted to use of deadly force, you are required to retreat rather than result to the use of deadly force in self defense, if a safe retreat is available, unless in the case under the "castle doctrine." For in such a situation, you may not leave your own home.

Finally, in the case where one started a murderous assault upon another or who willingly engaged in a mutual combat of a deadly nature and then changes his mind to end the encounter, such a person retains his right to self defense and has not lost it forever (See State v. Goode, *271, Mo. 43, 195 S.W. 1006[1917]*); but he has forfeited the privilege for the moment and may not reacquire it by "retreat to the wall." He must bring his attack to an end.[74] And if unable to get entirely away from his adversary, he must in some manner convey to him the information that the fight is over.[75] If circumstances do not permit him to do so this is his own misfortune for bringing such a predicament upon himself.[76]

---

[74] People v. Button, *106 Cal. 628, 39 P. 1073 (1895)*
[75] State v. Smith, *10 Nev. 106 (1875)*
[76] People v. Button, *106 Cal. 628, 39, P. 1073 (1895).*

PEOPLE V. LA VOIE

Supreme Court of Colorado
155 Colo. 551, 395 P.2d 1001 (1964)

The defendant was accused of the murder in information filed in the district court of Jefferson County. He entered a plea of not guilty and the case was brought before a jury. After all evidence was presented, the trial court, on motion of counsel for defendant, directed the jury to return the verdict of not guilty. It was the opinion of the trial court that due to insufficient evidence, there exists a clear case of justifiable homicide. The district attorney objected, and the case was submitted on a writ of error requesting the court to render an opinion expressing its disapproval of the trial court in directing the verdict of not guilty.

The defendant was a pharmacist at the Kincaid Pharmacy, 7024 West Colfax Avenue. Lakewood, Colorado. His day's work ended at about 12:30 A.M. After leaving work, he got something to eat at a nearby restaurant and went on his way home. He was driving east on West Colfax Avenue, toward the city of Denver, at about 1:30 A.M. An automobile approached his car from the rear. The driver of this auto made contact with the rear bumper of defendant's car and thereupon forcibly, unlawfully, and deliberately accelerated his motor, moving the defendant forward for a substantial distance and through a red traffic light. There were four men in the automobile who were intoxicated with liquor in varying degrees. Prior to ramming the car of the defendant they had agreed to shove him along just for "kicks." The defendant applied his brakes to the full; but the continuing force from behind precipitated him forward, causing all four wheels to leave a trail of skid marks.

When defendant's car finally stopped, the auto containing the four men backed away a few feet. The defendant got out of his car and as he did so he placed a revolver beneath his belt. He had a permit to carry the gun. The four men got out of their auto and advanced toward the defendant threatening to "make you eat that damn gun," to "mop up the street with you," and also directed vile, profane and obscene language at him. The man who was in advance of his three companions, moved toward defendant, in a menacing manner and at that point, the defendant shot him. As a result, he died at the scene of the affray.

In conclusion, the Supreme Court affirmed the not guilty verdict. In its opinion for the ruling, the court stressed the principle behind the law of justifiable homicide as set forth by the court in

Young v. People, 47 Colo. 352, 107 P. 274, where it was said that when a person has reasonable grounds for believing, and does in fact actually believe, that danger of being killed, or of suffering great bodily harm, is imminent, such person may act and defend himself, even to the extent of taking human life when necessary. He will not be at fault although it may turn out he had been mistaken as to the extent of the real or actual danger. In such situation, defendant had the right to defend himself.[77]

NOTES

[1] The right of homicide self-defense is available only to those free from fault. To hide under the cover of self-defense, you must not be the aggressor or instigator. However, this is not absolute for in some situations, you may still retain your right to act in self-defense depending on the facts. Nonetheless, the right of self-defense is denied to a slayer who incites the fatal attack, encourage the fatal quarrel or otherwise promote the necessitous occasion for taking life. Self-defense claim may not be justified if in fact, the claimant was the actual provoker. One who is the actual aggressor in a conflict causing death may not turn around to invoke the necessities of self-defense. However, if the aggressor has informed his adversary of his intention to quit and in good faith attempts to do so, he is restored to his right of self-defense. A homicide committed in self-defense is excusable only as a matter of genuine necessity.

[2] An affirmative unlawful act reasonably calculated to generate an affray leading to injury or fatal consequences is considered an aggression, which unless renounced nullifies the actor's right of homicide self-defense.

[3] **CASTLE DOCTRINE**: It is a settled principle of the law that one who through *no fault of his own* is attacked in his home, is under no duty to retreat therefrom.

[4] **RETREAT TO THE WALL**: One is not justified of using deadly force if other avenue of retreat is available to avoid a fatal response. The MPC provides that deadly force is not permissible if the actor knows he can avoid the necessity for employing deadly force, by surrendering possession of a thing to a person asserting the right to it or by complying with a demand that

---

[77] State v. Dwyer, *317 So.2d 149 (Fla.App.1975)* where Dwyer who was partially disabled by arthritis and hemmed in by a wall at his back and a bar at his side, was approached, by an alleged karate expert, who invited Dwyer to fight. As the assailant continued his charge upon Dwyer, Dwyer cut the other several times with a knife, inflicting injuries, which resulted in death. A conviction of manslaughter was reversed on the ground that this was justifiable self-defense.

he abstain from any action, which he has no duty to take. For example, the Model Penal Code outlaws the use of force against a known police officer, even when the arrest carried out by the officer is unlawful. This however, does not bar the use of force in self-defense if the officer uses excessive force in making the unlawful arrest.

[5] A non-deadly aggressor who started an encounter using only his fists or other forms of non-deadly weapon who is met with a deadly force in defense may justifiably defend himself against the deadly attack. If the aggressor in *good faith* decides to withdraw from further encounter with his victim, he must notify his victim of his intention to quit in order to make an effective withdrawal thereby, restoring his right to self-defense. The majority rule is that the defender who was not the original aggressor, need not retreat even though, he can do so safely before using deadly force upon an assailant whom he reasonably believe would kill him or do bodily harm.

[6] ***IMPERFECT SELF-DEFENSE***: This is the unreasonable belief in the need to act in self-defense, leading to a homicide. It may lower the crime from murder to voluntary manslaughter. Many states that have adopted the doctrine based on statutory law have subscribed to the *subjectively honest* but *objectively* unreasonable standard of the imperfect self-defense doctrine therefore, the defendant is not fully exculpated because the homicide was done without justification or excuse. However, one who lawfully acts in self-defense could not be criminally liable for unintentionally causing injury upon a bystander in doing so; but his action must not be the result of recklessness. The following is a question received in response to an article I wrote on self-defense titled: *Self Defense: A Settled Principle of Criminal Law*, available at http://www.san0670.com

QUESTION: *What happens if a simple and innocent action makes someone to be so afraid that he reacts, thinking he is in a serious danger. Suppose one dresses up one night as in Halloween, and decides to show it to a friend frightening him as a joke... What happens if the friend becomes so terrorized and afraid that he takes a gun or a knife to respond?*[78]

RESPONSE: *Normally, this is a case of imperfect self-defense in criminal law. If a homicide occurred as a result, the defendant might have acted based on unreasonable belief that his life was in danger. Such a situation will reduce the crime of murder to voluntary manslaughter and because the killing was committed without reasonable justification, the slayer will not be entitled to full exoneration. He will not be guilty of murder but could be charged with voluntary manslaughter depending on the facts of the case.*

---

[78] Comment and question by *Francisco Javier Teran*, Colegio Portaceli Seville, Spain (08/14/12).

[7] What is important when acting in self-defense, is the reasonableness of the actor's action. The defendant must show convincingly that he had a reasonable belief, as to the imminence of great bodily harm or death, which necessitates the force to compel it.

DEFENSE OF OTHERS

The law that gives one the right of self-defense also confers the privilege to act in defense of others whenever it is reasonable and necessary to do so. It would be unreasonable and unwise for a man to watch while his daughter or wife is being threatened in his presence with serious bodily harm or death, while he has the capability and privilege to prevent the harm, and when based on the circumstances that, his wife or daughter has the right of self-defense. "One may do in another's defense whatever the other might in the circumstances do for himself."[79]

The privilege to act in defense of others can be traced back to the law of property, where the right to act in defense of ones habitation and property, may be extended to the protection of ones wife, children and servants. Blood is ticker than water; family ties creates a special bond and association, which makes a man responsible for the welfare and protection of his wife, children and others with whom he enjoys special relationship and friendship. Any member of the family has the privilege to defend another member; the master has the right to defend his servant, or the servant defends the master.[80]

The privilege to act in defense of others in some cases may be based on the duty to do so. Normally, a father has the duty to protect his child, his wife and members of his immediate family whenever it is necessary and reasonable to do so; and in some situations, the privilege may be extended to members of the household or others whom he is under a legal or socially recognized duty to protect.[81] A failure to act in defense of another when there is a legal and recognized duty to do so can make the actor to be both criminally and civilly liable to the other, depending on the facts of the case. Thus a conductor is privileged to defend his passenger, and a person is privileged to defend a friend whom he is with at the moment.[82] In fact, in some situations, one may act in defense of a stranger when privileged to do so, (Salmond, *Torts 375 (11th Ed. 1953)*).

---

[79] Bishop, *Criminal Law § 877 (9th Edition 1923)*

[80] Pond v. People, *8 Mich. 150, 176 (1860)* A man may defend his family, his servants or his master, whenever he may defend himself.

[81] Restatement, Second, Torts § 76, Comments e, f (1965)

[82] Restatement, Second, Torts ibid

Despite the conferred privilege, the actor is required to act reasonably while doing so in defense of another; and just as in self-defense, he may not use deadly force in response to a non-deadly force to save another, and a non-deadly force must not be in excess of what is needed.[83] While acting in defense of another, it is essential the one using the privilege act reasonably by making sure the one he is acting to protect, is privileged to act in his own self- defense and in that case, the privilege is transferred to the actor. For example, if **A** the aggressor and instigator pulls out a dagger and about to stab **B** to death, and **B** knowing her life was about to be over, pulls a gun and takes aim to fire as **A** launches to stab her and **C**, **A**'s husband a sharp shooter, seeing the commotion from the window of his apartment, pulls his gun and shoots **B** to death to protect **A** his wife; can **C** claim the defense of other to avoid prosecution for the murder of **B**?

In most cases the answer is no for the following reasons: while **C** may have the privilege to act in defense of his wife in prescribed circumstances, he can only do so if his wife **A,** has the right to self-defense. In this case, **A** is the aggressor and instigator, she began the events that led to the trouble in the first place and not only that, she responded to a non-deadly encounter with a deadly force. She introduced the dagger (*deadly object*) and for that moment, she has lost her right to self-defense. Therefore, her husband **C** cannot act in her defense with a deadly force because for that moment the privilege no longer exists and cannot be transferred to him. **B** possessed the right to self-defense the moment **A** brandished a dagger with the intention to stab her to death; at that point **B** may respond with a deadly force of same magnitude (*a gun*). The only way **A** could regain her right to self-defense is if she decides to end the encounter right away by withdrawing the dagger and conveying to **B** her intention to end the fight right there; and if the circumstances do not permit her to do so, she may have acted at her own peril because for those split seconds, **B** has the right to either save her own life by acting in self-defense or die with a dagger to her heart.

In essence, **C** may be properly prosecuted for the murder of **B.** He was not in line of danger or fear for his own life, but acted on behalf of his wife with a deadly force, based on a privilege that no longer exists for the particular moment. Though, his intention was to save his wife's life, he may have acted recklessly and unreasonably causing the unjustifiable homicide of **B.** If **C** was in line of fire and acted to save his own life, the homicide would have been justified.

In **PEOPLE v. CURTIS,** *52 Mich. 616, 18 N.W. 385,* Curtis was tried in the Cass County Circuit Court and convicted of murder in the second degree. Errors are assigned on rulings during the trial and in instructions to the jury. Macon Wilson was the person killed. ...

---

[83] Ibid at comment b

The respondent was entitled and bound to take an interest in the life and safety of his brother. There was no difference in the testimony as to his being in danger, and all the instructions, which confined the right of respondent to helping him only when he was entirely without fault, were unwarranted. The court refused to charge that a brother might interpose against a felonious or serious bodily harm, unless the assailed party was entirely blameless, and this was contradictory to the well-settled principle that a dangerous felony may be prevented by one who is not himself in the wrong, directly or by complicity. ...[84]

The judgment was reversed and a new trial ordered. The court remanded the prisoner to the custody of the Sheriff of Cass County, and allowed bail if he desires it, in a moderate amount.

DEFENSE OF HABITATION

Normally, one has the right to defend his home and place of dwelling; a person is justified in using all force available and at his disposal, to prevent unlawful and forcible entry of another with the intent to cause an attack upon his habitation. To do so, he is only justified in using deadly force in most instances if: a forcible entry is effected in a violent or tumultuous manner and based on a reasonable belief, that the entry was done with the purpose to cause an assault or personal violence upon anyone in his dwelling.

The right to protect ones habitation is not limited to the home or place of residence alone, it may be extended to any place occupied for the moment or regarded as a substitute home or dwelling; this may include a hotel, motel or while a guest in the home of another.[85]

A man's habitation is considered his *"Castle"* and at common law the inhabitant is privileged to use deadly force if based on the circumstances, it seems reasonable and necessary, to deter the commission or consummation of a dangerous felony such as burglary. The dweller may also use deadly force if it seems necessary and reasonable, to prevent the commission of arson upon his habitation. He may do so with the sole purpose of saving the house itself from damage or destruction. (*State v. Edwards, 28 N.C.App. 196, 220 S.E.2d 158 (1975).*

Just as the owner or dweller is privileged to use deadly force when necessary and reasonable to do so, he is also privileged to use reasonable non-deadly force to prevent unlawful harm or injury to

---

[84] One may kill if necessary to save his brother's life even if the latter started the difficulty unless he did so with felonious intent. *Little v. State, 87 Miss. 512, 40 So. 165 (1906)*

[85] State v. Osborne, *200 S.C. 504, 21 S.E.2d 178 (1942)*

his dwelling. However, he is not privileged to deter any and every *trespass* with a deadly force; such a force may be used only when there is reasonable and justifiable belief there is danger of great bodily harm or peril to his person. (*People v. Eastman, 405 Ill. 491, 498, 91 N.E. 387, 390 (1950)*)

NOTE: *The right to protect ones habitation and dwellings confers no moral privilege to commit a homicide for that purpose, unless when it is necessary to do so.*

DEFENSE OF PROPERTY

Just as one may act reasonably in defense of his habitation, he is also privileged to defend his property with a non-deadly force, when it is reasonably necessary to do so. He may do so in protection of both real and personal property from unprivileged interference by others however, he must use force not in excess of that necessary in such a situation.[86] If his use of non-deadly force results in a homicide found to be accidental, his action does not constitute criminal homicide.[87]

It would be unreasonable for the owner to beat an intruder with the butt of a gun just for plucking an orange from his tree, just as it was held "unreasonable to beat an old man with a cane merely because he was picking a few flowers".[88] One who decides to beat another with the butt of a gun for plucking an orange, would be using unnecessary and excessive force. Beating with the butt of a gun is not a justifiable way of putting a mere trespasser out of his compound and if a death occurs as a result of his action, it would amount to criminal homicide, due to the unreasonable and unjustifiable use of excessive force. The owner may use reasonable force to eject a trespasser from his home, after notice to withdraw is ignored.[89]

The owner will not be justified to use deadly force to protect his property from mere interference, such a privilege is only available if an intrusion of his habitation is involved, and this is so even when the trespass cannot be prevented otherwise.[90] If the intruder's intent is to commit a felony in the dwelling, the owner may respond with the reasonable force necessary to the extent of the use of a deadly force; "But in the absence of an attempt to commit a felony, he cannot defend his property, except his habitation, to the extent of killing the aggressor for the purpose of preventing

---

[86] Carpenter v. State, 62 Ark. 286, 310, 36 S.W. 900, 907 (1896); A man may use force to defend his real or personal property in his actual possession against one who endeavors to dispossess him with right, taking care that the force used appears to be necessary for the purpose of defense and prevention.

[87] Morgan v. Durfree, 69 Mo. 469 (1987)

[88] Chapell v. Schmidt, *104 Cal. 511, 58 P. 892 (1894)*

[89] Phelps v. Arnold, *112 Cal.App. 518, 297 P. 31 (1931)*

[90] See *Turpen v. State, 89 Okl.Cr. 6, 204 P.2d 298 (1949)*

the trespass; and if he should do so, he would be guilty of a felonious homicide." (*Carpenter v. State, supra*).

The principle is based on the fact that life is precious and valuable than property and therefore, no one has the right to commit a homicide in defense of mere property, when a less extreme means is available to protect the property. But in an attempt to prevent an "unlawful entrance into a dwelling-house, the occupant may make defense to the taking of life, without being liable even for manslaughter." (*2 Bishop, Criminal Law § 707 (9ᵗʰ ed. 1923)*). In a case where the occupant reasonably believes the intruder intends to kill him, or cause a great bodily harm upon him, or upon a member of the household, "he may make his defense at the threshold;"[91] In that case, the defender is under no obligation to stay the use of a deadly force until the other has gained passage into his dwelling. However, the accepted view is that the use of deadly force is not permitted to prevent a relatively unimportant trespass.

In most cases, deadly force is only privileged when its use is reasonable and necessary to end the intruder's felonious intent to cause a great bodily harm or death to the defender; or when it is necessary to deter the intruder's unlawful and felonious act to cause a great damage to the property such as an attempt to commit arson upon the dwelling.

---

[91] *Bailey v. People 54 Colo. 337, 130 P. 832 (1913); Cro.Car. 554, 79 Eng.Rep. 1069 (K.B.1639)*

Adeyemi Oshunrinade

Notes: Answer the following questions choosing the right answers from the available choices.

Jenny was sleeping in her bedroom when she heard rumblings in her backyard. She proceeded to check and found Dan a stranger, trying to carry away her daughter's bicycle. She fired a shot and killed Dan instantly. At trial Jenny claimed she yelled, "stop thief!" before firing the fatal shot but evidence revealed that though, Dan attempted to steal the bicycle, no one heard Jenny say anything.

Charged with murder, the jury should be instructed that:

(A) Jenny was not privileged to use a deadly force unless she warned Dan
(B) Jenny was not privileged to use excessive force to prevent Dan's escape
(C) Jenny was privileged to use deadly force to protect her habitation at all times
(D) Jenny was not privileged to use deadly force to prevent the theft of her daughter's bicycle
(E) Jenny was privileged to stand her ground and use deadly force to end Dan's intrusion

Notes: Same facts as you have above. Assume the jury concluded that Jenny's use of deadly force is unprivileged.

Which of the following choices best describe how the jury came to the conclusion?

    (A) The use of deadly force is only limited to misdemeanors

    (B) Use of deadly force is only necessary to stop a fleeing pickpocket

    (C) Use of deadly force is only limited to felonies that involve a substantial risk of death or serious bodily harm

    (D) Use of deadly force is only necessary to stop a non-dangerous crime

    (E) None of the above

When Maya realized that his boyfriend was leaving her for Veronica another neighborhood girl, she decided it was time to settle issues once and for all. Armed with a gun borrowed from her friend, she went to Veronica's house, held her at gun- point and told her to say her last prayer because she could no longer share her boyfriend with her. Veronica begged for her life, while Maya tied her up and aimed the gun at her head. Just as the commotion was going on, Kane an active police office and Veronica's brother arrived home for the day. Maya spun around still holding the gun when she heard his footsteps. The sight of the gun scared Kane as he quickly drew his gun and fired at Maya killing her instantly.

If Kane is charged with murder of Maya, what defense(s) best support his case?

    (A) Defense of habitation

    (B) Self-defense

    (C) Defense of others

    (D) (B) And (C) above

Notes: A new scenario below, read the question and find the appropriate choice from the list provided.

Johnny a retired police officer and single father, was on his way to the high security company where he worked the graveyard shift as an armed guard, when he realized he had left his ID at home and won't be able to get in the office without it. He called home to have his 17-year-old daughter Catherine, bring the ID and meet him half way so, he won't drive all the way home. There was no response despite several calls. He thought this was unusual and decided to drive all the way back home. At the entrance to Catherine's bedroom he could hear a big struggle. Sam a registered sex offender was right on top of Catherine and about to rape her. Sam lifted a vase on the bedside table ready to smash it on Catherine's head to end her struggle but just that moment, two shots rang out. Sam's body was later recovered in a pool of blood. Jonny had shot him twice with his official revolver to prevent the rape and possible death of Catherine.

What crime is Johnny guilty of?

(A) Murder for failing to call 911
(B) Murder for using a deadly weapon to end a mere rape
(C) Not guilty for using a deadly weapon to end a dangerous felony
(D) Manslaughter since he did not premeditate Sam's death
(E) (A) And (B) above

Same situation as you have in the question above. Imagine that Jonny is found not guilty and answer the question below.

IF Johnny is found not guilty, what possible defense(s) could help his case?

    (A) Defense of property
    (B) Self-defense
    (C) Defense of others
    (D)(A) And (B) above
    (E) None of the above

Imagine you are the attorney for Johnny write a one page argument in the space below describing what defense is appropriate and why Johnny should not be found guilty of any crime?

On Christmas Eve 2001, Steve, John and Michael, were drinking and playing games in a bar when Joe an old friend walked in. All three have been friends since their High School days but things turned sour for John and Joe few years back when Joe refused to lend John some money he badly needed. Steve beckoned to Joe and asked if he could buy him a bottle of Heineken but Joe refused since he thought Steve and Michael had conspired with John to hate him. Steve became infuriated and started attacking Joe for refusing his request for a bottle of Heineken. The beating became very violent and unbearable for Joe so, he yelled for help and begged the others to please stop Steve before something bad happens. Instead of helping, John who was still angry with Joe for refusing to lend him money encouraged Steve to beat Joe more. "I'm not going to help you, I hope he beats the hell out of you this time, beat the life out of him Steve," he said. Michael on the other hand stood by and watched as Steve continued to beat Joe until Joe became unconscious. Joe was rushed to the hospital but died on arrival.

You are the attorney for John and he has been charged along with Steve for murder of Joe. How do you intend to defend your client? Do you think a murder charge is proper in this case and what defense if any does John have? Please write your arguments in a lengthy essay below.

Assume the fact remains as described above. If John is charged with First Degree murder of Joe, John is:

(A) Guilty, because he knew Steve was going to kill Joe and he continued to encourage him

(B) Guilty because he wished that Steve would kill Joe since Joe refused to lend him money

(C) Not guilty, because he did not participate and had no hand in Joe's beating death

(D) Not guilty of First Degree murder but guilty of a lesser charge of homicide

(E) None of the above

Imagine that John is charged with Second Degree murder of Joe, he is:

(A) Guilty as charged

(B) Not guilty at all

(C) Only guilty of battery

(D) Not guilty but only liable for aiding Joe

(E) None of the above

Same fact pattern as stated above, now, imagine that Joe did not die but was badly wounded from the b\eatings. Which of the followings can John be properly charged with?

(A) Battery of Joe

(B) Aiding and abetting

(C) Criminal contempt

(D) Failing to help his friend Joe

(E) (A) And (B) above

On a charge of battery of Joe, John is:

(A) Not guilty, because John had no legal duty to help Joe

(B) Not guilty, because failing to help a crime victim does not make one guilty

(C) Not guilty, because he did not participate or assist in the commission of battery

(D) Guilty, because he was aware Steve was attempting to physically beat Joe but yet, he encouraged Steve to beat Joe

(E) None of the above

Note: In any crime, a witness to the offense who aids, counsels, encourages and command the principal in the first degree, is considered a principal in the second degree for all purposes. All participants in a crime so as to share liability for the offense are referred to as accomplices. The actions performed by an accomplice are called "aiding and abetting," and the mental state needed for an accomplice liability is described as acting with the purpose to encourage or help the principal accomplish his criminal motive.

Scott asked Darren to loan him $200,000. As security for the loan, Scott entered into an agreement to give his beautiful house to Darren if for any reason he could not pay him back. A Mexican drug lord was threatening Scott for failing to remit the $200,000 he owed him as part of a deal they had. Scott knew not paying back the drug lord could mean his demise so he approached Darren, for the loan. Darren wanted Scott's house but could not afford the $700,000 price tag so he thought this might be his opportunity to own it if Scott fails to pay up. From day one Scott had no intention of paying Darren back. He knew he could not pay him back but he needed the money badly and was not ready to lose his priced home for just $200,000. Scott concocted a plan to have Darren killed, he hired an assassin to do the job, provided the gun and paid for the service. Two days before payment is due, Darren was found dead killed execution style. The hired assassin entered into a deal and was sentenced to fifty years for his cooperation.

You are the attorney general for the borough and you have been asked to prosecute the case. Write a brief of how you plan to argue the case before a jury and against the defense. What charge or charges are proper against Scott? What arguments best support a possible murder charge in this case?

Based on the facts of the case, Scott is guilty of:

> **(A) First degree murder**
> **(B) Second degree murder**
> **(C) Manslaughter**
> **(D) Conversion for taking Scott's money**
> **(E) Conspiracy to commit murder**

The defense, has argued that Scott should be guilty of Second Degree murder, you believe the charge is proper because:

> **(A) Scott did not carry out the shooting, assassin did**
> **(B) Scott had no time to think about the shooting he only paid assassin who went ahead to kill Darren**

(C) Scott had no choice and since his life was threatened, he must do whatever necessary to pay back drug lord

(D) (A) And (B) above

(E) None of the above

If Scott if found guilty and convicted of First Degree murder, the best argument would be that:

(A) Scott intended the death of Darren

(B) Scott premeditated and deliberated the death of Darren

(C) Scott hired assassin to kill Darren

(D) Scott provided the gun for Darren's murder

(E) (A) And (B) above

Imagine that Darren did not die but Scott tricked him into believing he would pay him back but took the money with the intention not to pay Darren. In such a situation, Scott can be successfully charged with:

(A) Embezzlement

(B) Conversion

(C) Larceny by trick depending on whether or not the jurisdiction considers money property

(D) Burglary

(E) (A), (B) And (C) above

(F) None of the above

Abbot had recently separated from his wife Abby, he was depressed and heartbroken about the separation and wanted to get back with Abby. After drinking a lot of Vodka and intoxicated, he went to Abby's house banging on the door and yelling at her to open the door immediately. When Abby refused to let him in, Abbot broke the door and began cursing Abby and yelling at her. Abby became angry and cursed back at Abbot for getting too abusive. Abbot became infuriated, picked up a metallic elephant statue on the table and threw it at Abby. The object struck Abby's head killing her instantly.

You have been hired to defend Abbot in a First Degree murder charge. What defense are you most likely to assert? What are the possibilities your client cannot be guilty as charged? Is there any likelihood that your client is relieved of criminal liability?

Based on the facts above, which of the following defense(s) are available to Abbot?

    (A) Self-defense

    (B) Defense of others

    (C) Abbot's action is protected under the "stand your ground rule"

    (D) Intoxication

    (E) Self-defense and intoxication

    (F) None of the above

If Abbot asserts the defense of intoxication, part of the Jury's instruction must be that:

    (A) Abbot should go free without liability because alcohol destroyed his reasoning

    (B) Abbot is not liable for Abby's death, because alcohol made him incapable of knowing right from wrong when he attacked Abby

    (C) Abbot's intoxication should not be mitigated since he voluntarily consumed alcohol

    (D) Abbot's intoxication does not mean total relief from criminal liability, but it could be enough to negate his ability to premeditate and deliberate Abby's death, such that his crime is mitigated to Second degree murder from murder first

    (E) None of the above

Officers Paton and Jason, received call via 911 that Devon a 19-year-old teen had assaulted two of his neighbors and was about to beat the third one up. They approached Devon and informed him he was under arrest for the assault but Devon refused to comply and instead, ran away from the officers. Both officers pursued Devon on foot with the intention to carry out the arrest. As they approached a street corner, Devon suddenly turned around, faced the officers and started hurling stones at them. Both officers opened fire, releasing a total of five shots that killed Devon. Evidence revealed Paton fired 3 shots and Jason 2. The fatal shot to the head came from Jason's gun, which Forensic evidence showed killed Devon.

If charged with Second Degree murder, both officers are equally:

(A) **Guilty for killing an unarmed teen**

(B) **Only Jason is guilty for firing the fatal shot**

(C) **Not guilty, officers acted in self-defense**

(D) **Guilty for failing to use a less deadly force**

(E) **None of the above**

If both officers are found not guilty, the best argument they have is that:

(A) **They acted accordingly to arrest a fleeing criminal**

(B) **They acted in self-defense since a stone is considered a deadly weapon**

(C) **They had no other choice but to shoot Devon since he resisted arrest**

(D) **(B) And (C) above**

(E) **Only (A) And (B)**

Matt a Georgian police officer responding to reports of a suspicious person, shot and killed Cedric an unarmed man who was banging on people's doors and running around naked in a metro Atlanta apartment complex. Matt fired two shots when Cedric charged at him and refused to stop as ordered by officer Matt. Cedric was killed at the scene and evidence later revealed he was unarmed, when he charged at officer Matt. Further investigation showed that before the incident, Cedric was acting deranged, knocking on doors and crawling around naked. When officer Matt arrived, he called Cedric to stop but when he failed to obey his orders and charged at him, officer Matt stepped backward, drew his weapon and fired two shots at Cedric. Forensic investigation revealed that Cedric was shot twice in the upper body and medical records showed he suffered from some mental health issues before the incident. During the incident, officer Matt had access to his stun gun and pepper spray, but it is unknown why he chose to draw his weapon.

Officer Matt has been charged with First Degree murder for killing Cedric an unarmed man.

If prosecuted as charged, officer Matt is likely to be found:

(A) **Guilty**

(B) **Not guilty**

(C) **Guilty of the felony murder of Cedric**

(D) **Guilty of manslaughter**

(E) None of the above

If not charged with First Degree murder which of the followings crimes, can officer Matt, be charged with? Select the most likely charge possible:

(A) Second degree murder
(B) Voluntary manslaughter
(C) Involuntary manslaughter
(D) Battery
(E) Negligent homicide

Imagine that officer Matt is convicted of the negligent homicide of Cedric, which of the followings may help the Jury reach their decision:

(A) Officer Matt acted irresponsibly when he chose to fire at Cedric
(B) Officer Matt failed to calm down Cedric when he should have done so
(C) Officer Matt had no right to shoot though, Cedric charged at him
(D) Officer Matt used excessive force when he should have used a reasonable and less deadly force
(E) None of the above

Patton pointed his newly acquired Colt 45 at his friend Tim jokingly, but suddenly, the gun went off and Tim is killed. If prosecuted for the murder of Tim, Patton will most likely be exculpated if:

(A) Patton had no inkling the gun was loaded
(B) Patton believed the gun was not loaded
(C) Patton did not intend the death of Tim and believed the gun was not loaded
(D) Patton believed the gun was unloaded and had a reasonable belief
(E) (A), (B) And (C)

If Patton had a genuine belief that the gun was unloaded, then:

(A) He had knowledge the gun might be loaded

(B) He acted with malice for aiming a gun in jest

(C) He lacked the requisite intent to kill

(D) He failed to exercise care

(E) None of the above

Angel was practicing shooting with his collection of rifles in a desert like vacant field not far from his home. Kids go to the same field to play little league baseball and several times, Angel was told to stop shooting there because of kids playing. On a beautiful Sunday morning, Angel set up target at one end of the field but quickly noticed some of the neighborhood kids were also playing baseball at the other end. He had a routine and planned to practice shooting that day so, he was not ready to let any sport events change his plans. Angel began firing at the targets, but one of his shots missed and struck one of the kids playing baseball. The kid died on arrival at the hospital.

If prosecuted, Angel is:

(A) Guilty of involuntary manslaughter

(B) Negligent homicide

(C) No crime, he only acted negligently

(D) Guilty of murder

(E) Voluntary manslaughter

Assume that Angel is found guilty of murder, which of the followings supports a murder conviction in this case:

(A) Angel committed an act demonstrating a depraved heart

(B) Angel engaged in extremely negligent conduct, which a reasonable person should know presents a high risk of death or bodily harm

(C) Angel engaged in a reckless conduct

(D) Angel acted with knowledge that children were around and his reckless conduct caused the death of another

(E) (A) (B) And (D) above

(F) All of the above

Ms. Wilson, an Elementary School Math teacher decided she had reached the end of the road and could no longer take life situations. She thought suicide was the only way out but did not want to die alone in the house. She wanted to die with other people present so, on a beautiful Monday morning, she placed a new revolver she just purchased in her handbag and went to school as usual. While in the staff room in front of other teachers, Ms. Wilson suddenly put the revolver in her own mouth and tried to pull the trigger. Mr. Fitzgerald, another teacher in the school, reached for the gun and struggled to pull it out of Ms. Wilson's mouth. As she continued to try and point the gun at herself, the gun went off. A bullet struck and killed Mr. Fitzgerald instantly.

If charged, Ms. Wilson is guilty of:

(A) Depraved heart murder, because in her attempt to commit suicide, she created a high risk of serious injury or death to anyone who might attempt to prevent the suicide
(B) No crime, since she only attempted to kill herself and had no intention of killing Mr. Fitzgerald
(C) Manslaughter, because a suicide attempt made with bystanders nearby is generally considered reckless conduct enough for involuntary manslaughter
(D) Intent to kill murder, since her intent to kill herself is transferred to Mr. Fitzgerald
(E) None of the above

If charged with First Degree murder, which of the following is true:

(A) Her attempt to commit suicide is sufficient as intent to kill Mr. Fitzgerald
(B) Her intent to commit suicide was premeditated at home and therefore, sufficient to find her guilty of Mr. Fitzgerald's death
(C) She knew someone would attempt to stop her and therefore, should be liable for First Degree murder
(D) A charge of First Degree murder will not stand since she lacked the requisite intent to kill Mr. Fitzgerald
(E) (B) And (C) above

Bob came home after a day of hard work and found that his life savings of $10,000 was missing from the safe. He became so angry but as he was about to call 911 to report the theft, Jack a neighbor whom Bob did not know, hate Gonzalez and had his own reasons for wanting Gonzalez dead, sent Bob an anonymous note telling him that it was Gonzalez who stole his money and that he saw him breaking into his home and leaving with a bag full of cash. Jack provided information on where to find Gonzalez and for three weeks, Bob planned and purchased a gun for his mission. Armed with the gun, Bob went on a search for Gonzalez but could not locate him until six weeks later. He was determined to get his money back or finish up Gonzalez. After a heated argument in which Bob accused Gonzalez of stealing his money and Gonzalez denied the allegations with alibi, Bob shot Gonzalez in the head.

Gonzalez was rushed to a hospital, where doctors determined that he was brain dead and he was placed on life support. Follow-up studies by the hospital confirmed he had lost all brain activities sufficient to declare him legally dead. Four days after, the medical team decided to disconnect the life support system and Gonzalez was pronounced dead.

Bob and Jack have been charged with murder and both were convicted. The prosecutor claimed that the murder was premeditated, willful, deliberate and done during the commission of felonious assault with a deadly weapon. Jack has also been charged with aiding and abetting Bob in killing Gonzalez. Both Bob and Jack have appealed. How should the appellate court rule on Bob's argument that:

(a) Evidence established that the decision of the medical team to remove life-support killed Gonzalez
(b) The court erred by instructing on murder in the commission of a felony
(c) The court should have instructed on Manslaughter not murder

How should the court of appeal rule on Jack's argument that:

(a) There is insufficient evidence to find him guilty as an aider and abettor
(b) The evidence is lacking to find him guilty of First Degree murder, when he did not fire the shot that killed Gonzalez

Your answers to the questions above, requires an essay format. All discussions must be supported with evidence from the facts of the case and must demonstrate that the student understands the laws that apply.

Based on the facts of the case, the following multiple choices questions are designed to guide and help you in finding the correct answers to the essay questions above.

In order for Bob's argument to succeed that physician's action to remove life support, caused Gonzalez's death:

(A) Bob must show that physician not Bob was the cause of death
(B) That Gonzalez was only pronounced dead after life-support was removed
(C) That Gonzalez would live had life-support not been removed
(D) That "but for" the removal of life-support, Gonzalez would survive
(E) All the above
(F) None of the above

Note: A defendant's action, will be the actual cause, if it is a "but for" cause of the result or at least a "substantial contributory factor" causing death.

To find Bob liable for Gonzalez's death, it must be established that:

(A) Bob's shot killed Gonzalez
(B) "But for" Bob's act of shooting Gonzalez in the head, he would not have died
(C) "But for" Bob's shooting, Gonzalez would not have been placed on life support
(D) Bob's action is the proximate cause of death
(E) (A), (B) And (C)
(F) All of the above

For Bob's argument that the court erred in its instruction on felony murder to succeed:

(A) Bob must show he was not engaged or attempted to engage in the perpetration of an inherently dangerous felony, when he shot Gonzalez
(B) That his only intent was to assault Gonzalez with a deadly weapon, which by itself is not enough to support a felony murder conviction
(C) That his intent to assault Gonzalez with a deadly weapon was not independent of the actual killing
(D) That a felony murder conviction would be proper if he had committed an independent felony other than the killing of Gonzalez

(E) All of the above

(F) None of the above

For Bob's argument on manslaughter instruction to succeed, he must show that:

(A) He acted out of anger as a result of legally adequate provocation

(B) He was subjectively angry enough to kill and a reasonable person would have been so angry to kill

(C) A reasonable person would still be angry to kill six weeks after his cash went missing though, he had time to "cool off"

(D) Mere denial by Gonzalez that he did not take the money, that is "words alone," would not be enough to stop a reasonable person from killing

(E) (A), (B) And (D) above

(F) All of the above

Note: When a defendant aids, encourages or offers support for another to commit a crime, such a defendant will also be guilty of the crime committed, if the defendant intends that the one aided will commit the crime. It is no defense that the defendant did not physically participate in the proscribed action.

To deny Jack's argument against his conviction for aiding and abetting, it must be established that:

(A) Jack provided the necessary aid to affect Bob's commission of the killing

(B) Jack had the requisite intent because he wanted Gonzalez dead

(C) Jack provided sufficient information that led to the location of Gonzalez and his eventual death

(D) All of the above

(E) (A) And (B) only

(F) None of the above

On Jack's conviction for First Degree murder, to find him guilty as charged:

(A) Jack must be liable as an accomplice to Bob

(B) Jack must have aided and abetted Bob in the commission of the crime

(C) Jack must intend Gonzalez's death and encourage it though he did not participate physically

(D) (B) And (C) only

(E) All of the above

(F) None of the above

Note: To properly answer the essay part of this question, be aware the Jury was instructed on the Felony Murder rule. Should that instruction alone be sufficient for overturning the murder conviction?

Selected Publications

Wayne R. Lafave, *Modern Criminal Law: Cases, Comments and Questions, 4th edition (2006)*

Rollin M. Perkins, et al, *Criminal Law and Procedure 6th edition (1984)*

William Prosser, *Law of Torts, 4th edition (1971)*

Nelson E. Roth & Scott E. Sundby, *The Felony Murder Rule: A Doctrine of Constitutional Crossroads (1985)*

Joseph J. Volpe, M.D., *Effect of Cocaine Use on the Fetus, 327 NEW ENG. J. MED. 399 (1992)*

Selected Cases

The following cases on homicide are specifically selected to help the student understand homicide law as a branch of criminal law. All cases are product of research and acquired accordingly.

Hughes v. State
Whitner v. State
Mullaney v. Wilbur
People v. Washington
People v. Berry
State v. Guthrie
State v. Snowden
State v. Hardie
State v. Bier
State v. Sety
Conrad v. State
State v. Losey
People v. Lewis
Kibbe v. Henderson
State v. Sauter
Limicy v. State
Smallwood v. State
People v. Roper
M'Naghten's Case
Davis v. State
Burrow v. State
Montana v. Egelhoff
Hubbard v. Commonwealth
Regina v. Holland
Commonwealth ex rel. Wadsworth v. Shortall
Viliborghi v. State
People v. La Voie
People v. Curtis